GREAT BOOK
MAZES

ROGER MOREAU

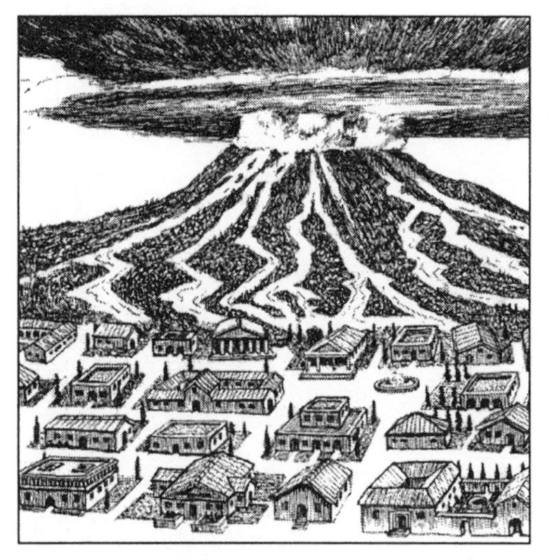

Sterling Publishing Co., Inc.
New York

10 9 8 7 6 5 4 3

Published by Sterling Publishing Company, Inc.
387 Park Avenue South, New York, N.Y. 10016

Distributed in Canada by Sterling Publishing
c/o Canadian Manda Group, One Atlantic Avenue, Suite 105
Toronto, Ontario, Canada M6K 3E7
Distributed in Great Britain and Europe by Chris Lloyd
463 Ashley Road, Parkstone, Poole, Dorset, BH14 0AX, England
Distributed in Australia by Capricorn Link (Australia) Pty Ltd.
P.O. Box 6651, Baulkham Hills, Business Centre, NSW 2153, Australia
Manufactured in the United States of America

CONTENTS

GREAT ESCAPE MAZES

CONTENTS

Introduction

There are many kinds of escapes. You could be held captive in prison against your will or trapped by enemy forces. You could be at the mercy of nature or a hostile environment through accident or misadventure. Often death will be the ultimate penalty, unless you can escape through your own efforts or are rescued by others. An escape or rescue from any of these circumstances always involves courage, risk and danger.

Throughout history, there have been many great escapes, and some of the greatest occurred during the twentieth century. Thanks to historians, photographers and the media, most of them have been well documented and details can be found in books and libraries. You will learn about some of these escapes here, and you will even have a chance to be involved in the rescues and experience the difficulties of the escape that took place. Hopefully, you will be successful and have the same kind of determination and courage that those involved in the real escapes had. It is also hoped that the day will never come when you find yourself in a situation where you really have to escape.

Now turn this page and go forth to be a part of some of the greatest escapes of the twentieth century.

Crash of the *Italia*

In 1928, Umberto Nobile attempted to fly over the north pole in the semi-rigid

Italia, but high winds broke the airship apart and the gondola crashed onto the ice. The survivors set up the famous "red tent" in the hope that it would be seen easily by rescuers. Find your way from the crash and set up the red tent.

Search for the Red Tent

Several attempts were made to locate the wreck, including one fatal one. Roald

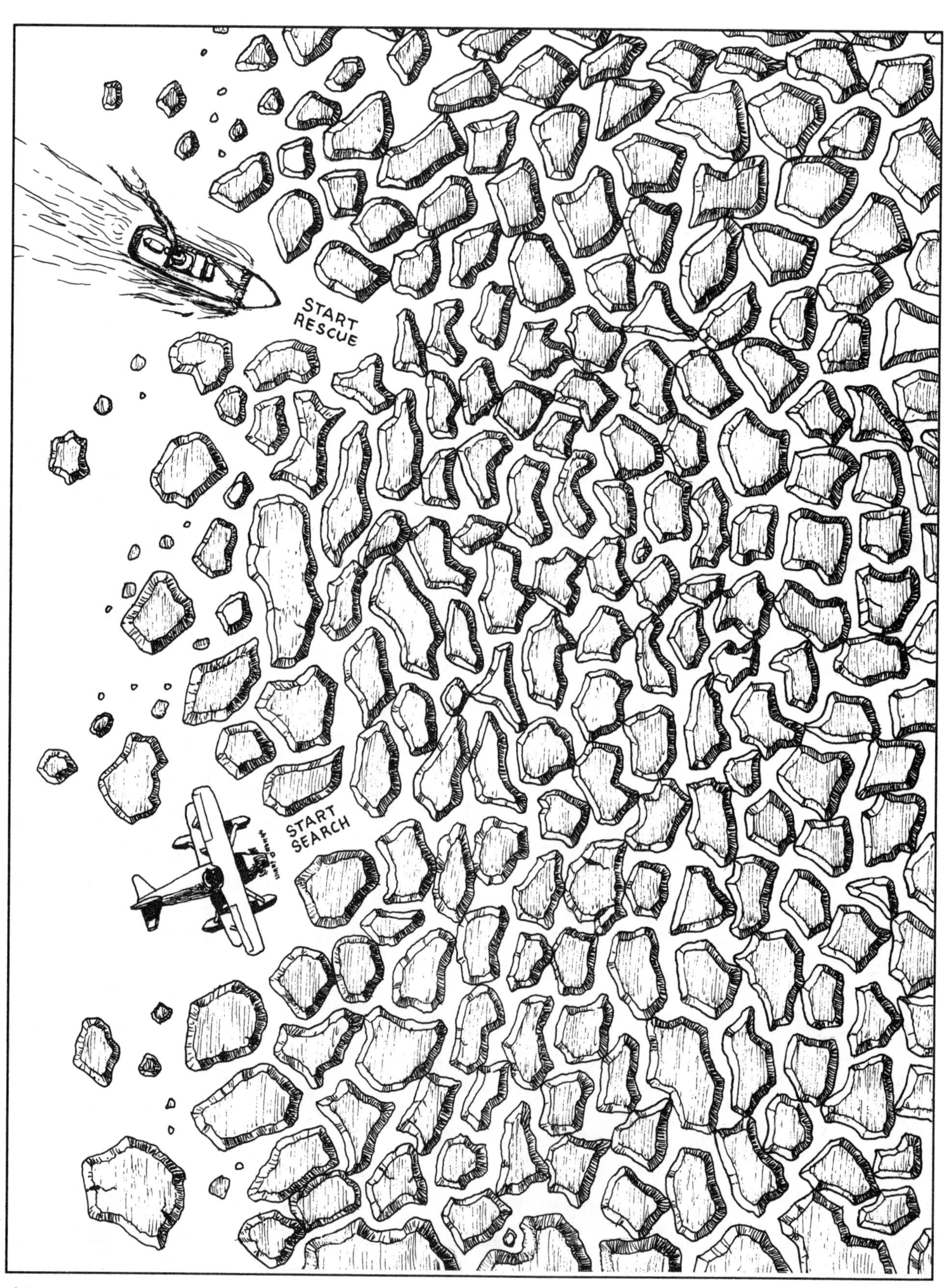

Amundsen, who had flown over the pole with Nobile in 1926, went down and was never heard from again. Use the seaplane to search for Nobile and his men in the red tent. When you find them, sail the ship in through the ice for the rescue.

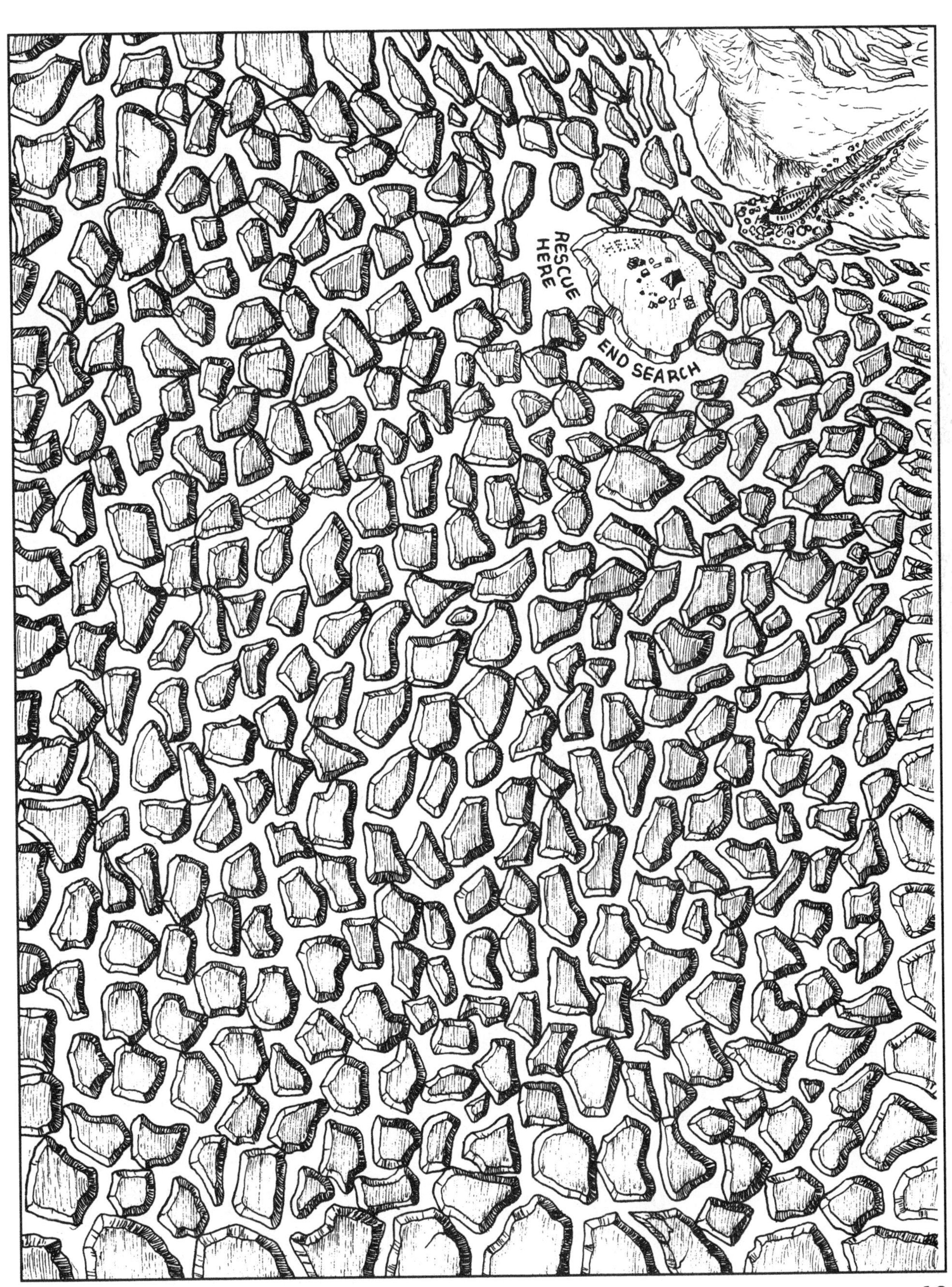

The *Hindenburg* Explodes

In May 1936, the *Hindenburg* airship, filled with hydrogen, caught fire as it was

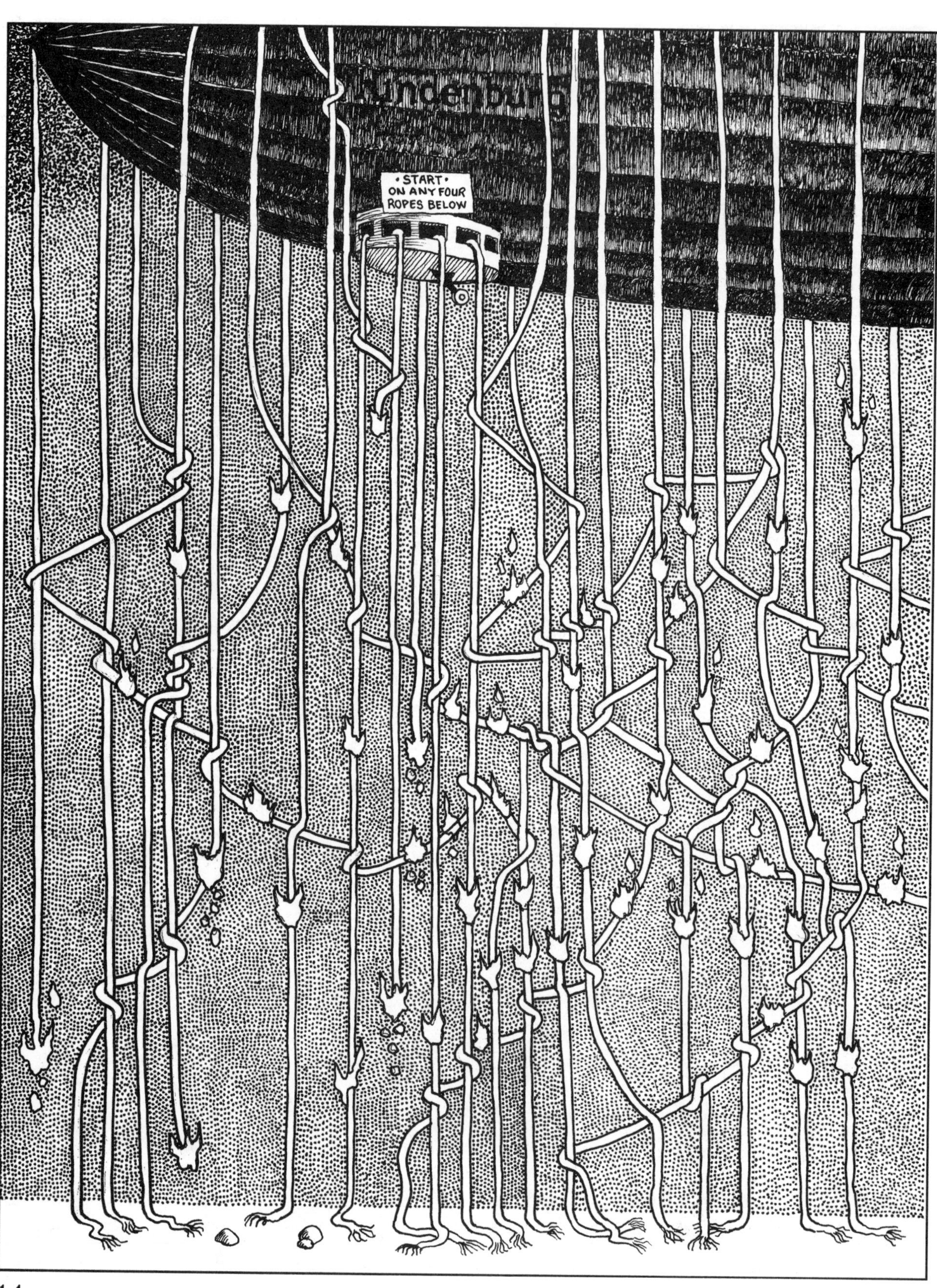

landing in New Jersey at the end of its maiden voyage. Escape the exploding air-ship by climbing down the ropes from the gondola. You can move from rope to rope where they touch, but avoid spots where the rope is burning. Hurry!

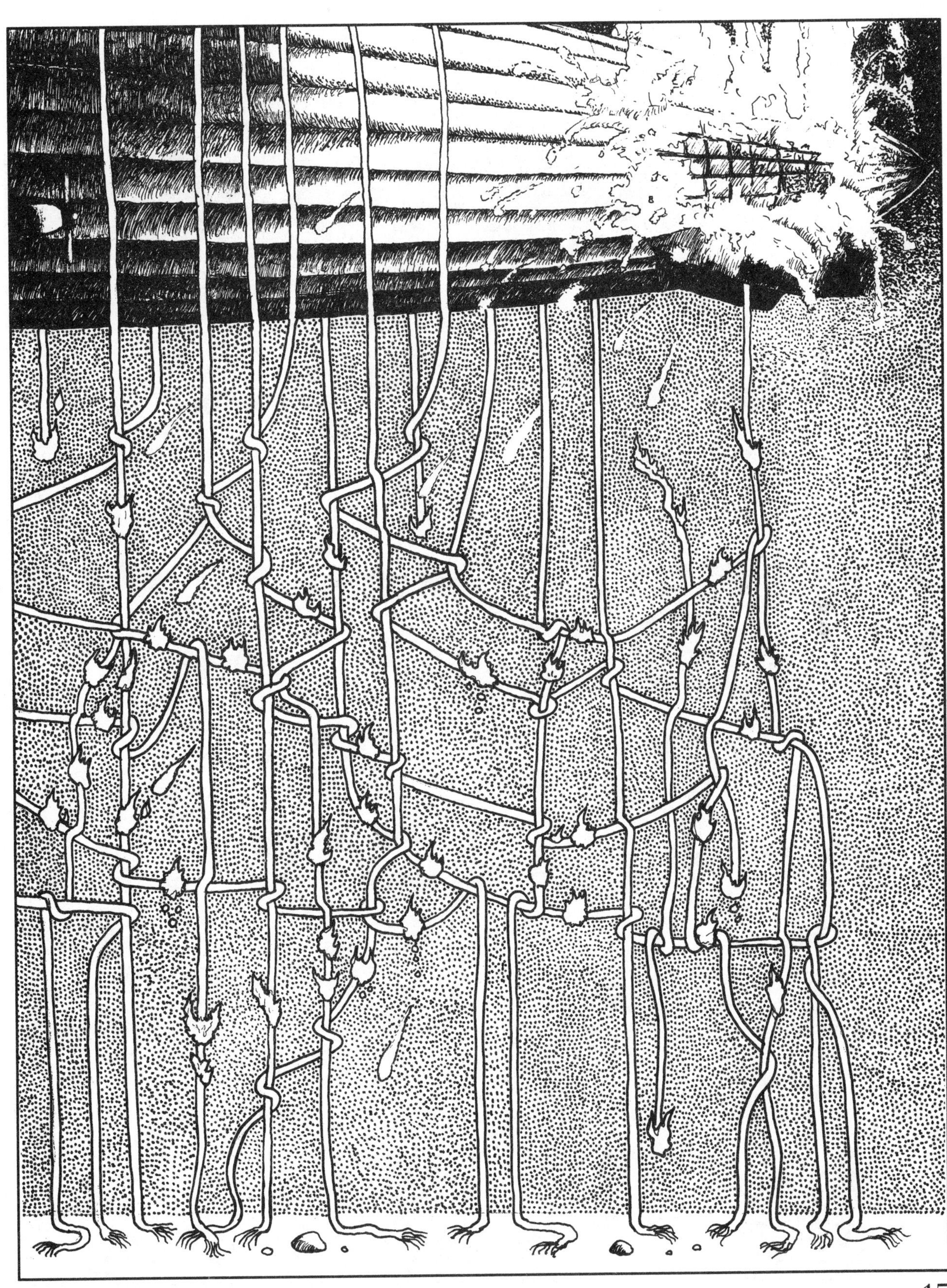

The *Squalus* Is Down

In 1939, when the U.S. submarine *Squalus* sank during testing in 240 feet of water

in Portsmouth, New Hampshire, harbor, she had over 50 men trapped in her hull. An experimental rescue diving bell was sent to the scene. Can you help guide the bell to the sub. Watch out for the school of cod that are swimming by.

"Houston, We Have a Problem"

Apollo 13 suffered severe damage on its way to the moon in 1970, and the crew

had to shut down the service module. They moved into the lunar module and had to conserve oxygen and fuel for nearly six and a half days. Help them find their way home by moving through the gaps.

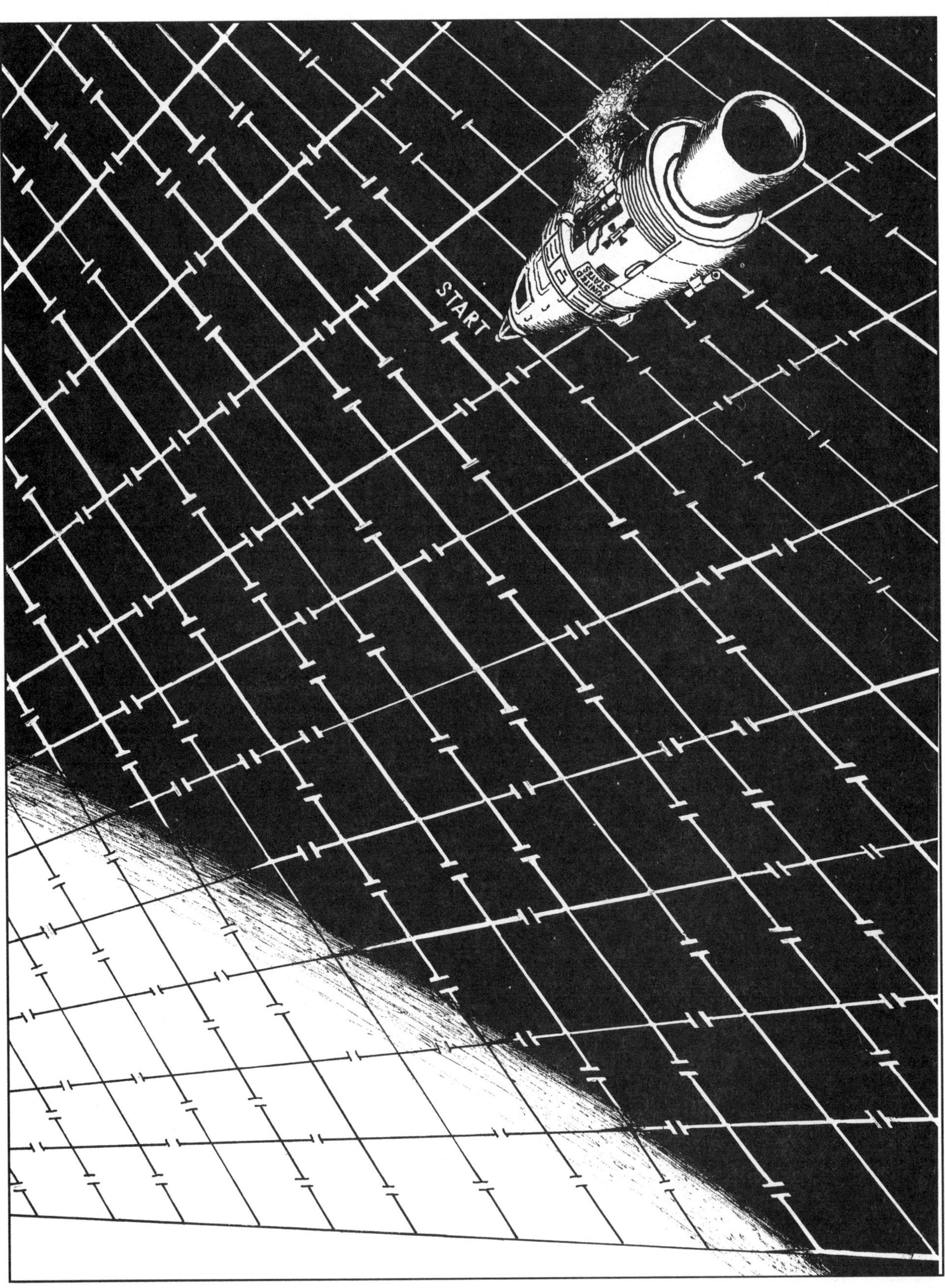

Crash in the Andes

In 1972, a plane crashed in the Andes Mountains with forty-five people on

board. Search efforts failed. Ten weeks after the crash, however, two survivors managed to hike out for help. Help them find their way by locating a clear path down the mountain.

Escape from Dunkirk

In 1940, nearly 400,000 Allied troops were trapped on the beach at Dunkirk in France

by advancing German forces and bombarded with heavy fire from the German air force. Most were evacuated by a huge flotilla of military, commercial, fishing, and pleasure boats. Help the troops find a clear path to the boats on the beach.

We Must Sink the *Bismarck*

Help the *Ark Royal*'s biplanes find the German battleship *Bismarck* for a torpedo run. Next, guide shells from the *Repulse, Rodney* and *King George V* to sink the ship.

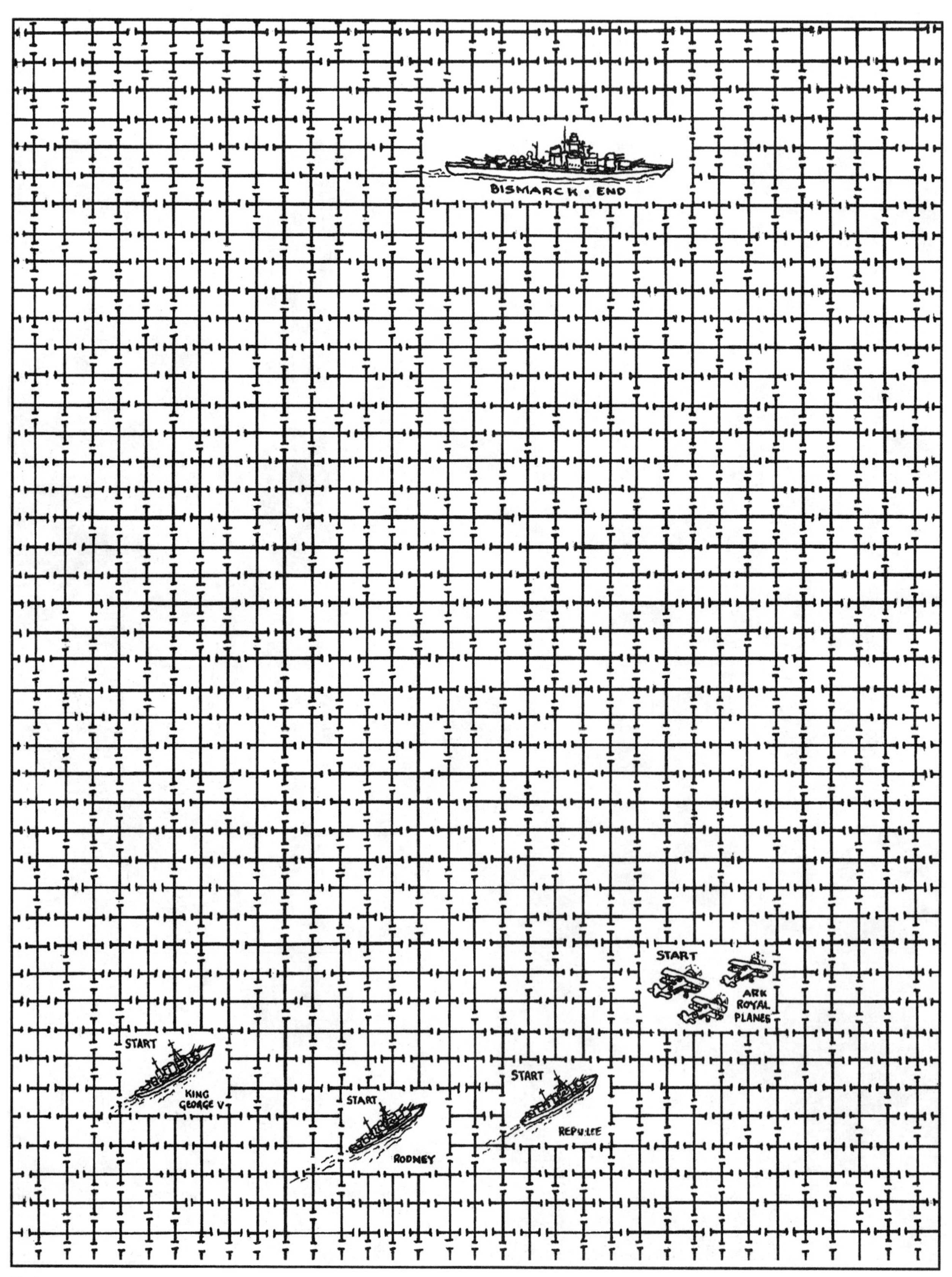

Doolittle's Raiders Down Behind Enemy Lines

After a bombing raid on Japan early in 1940, Doolittle's B-25 bombers had to ditch in occupied China. Help the fliers find a path to freedom. Do not pass a Japanese flag.

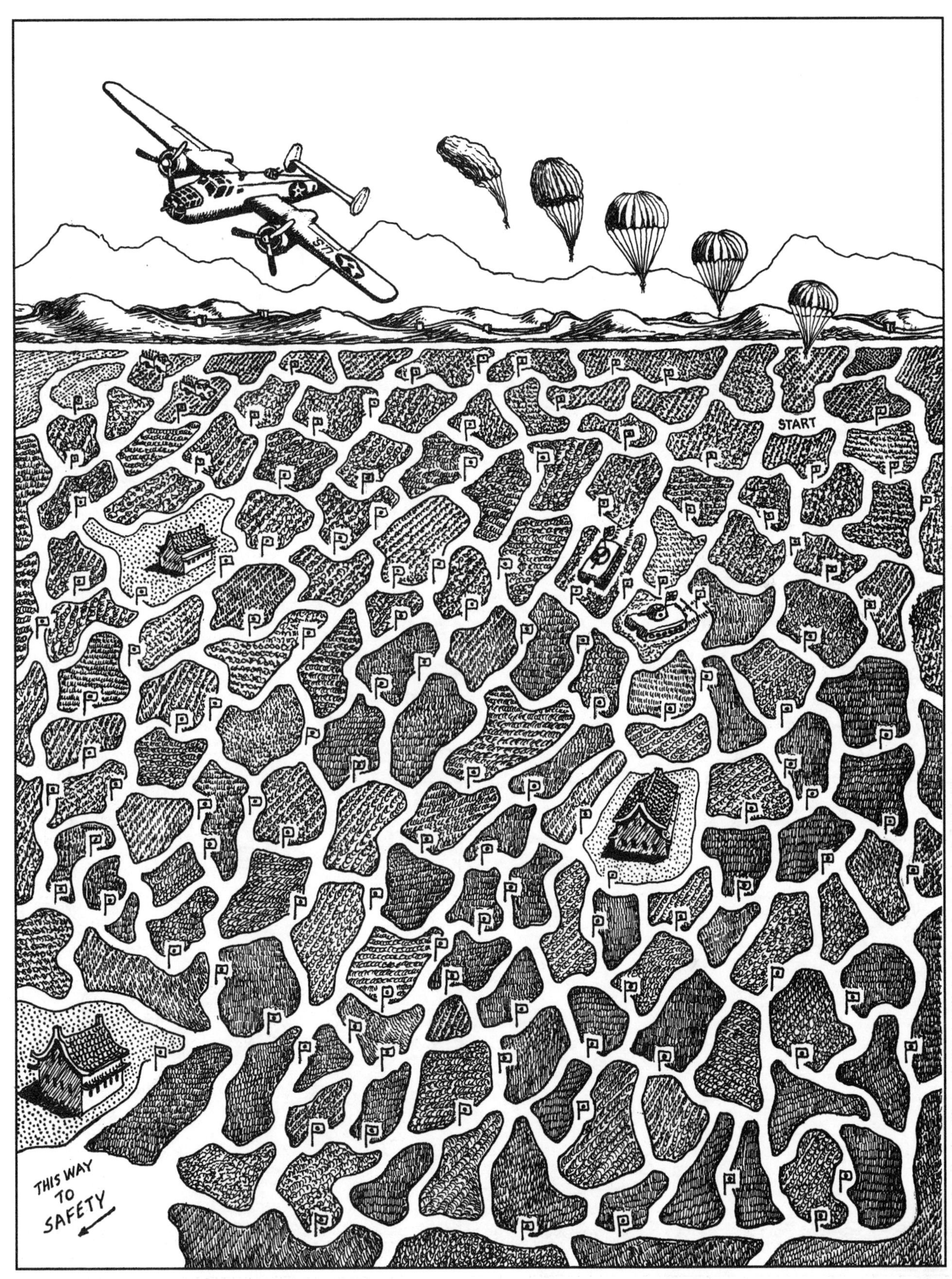

The Great Escape

One of the greatest escapes of World War II was from the German prisoner-of-war

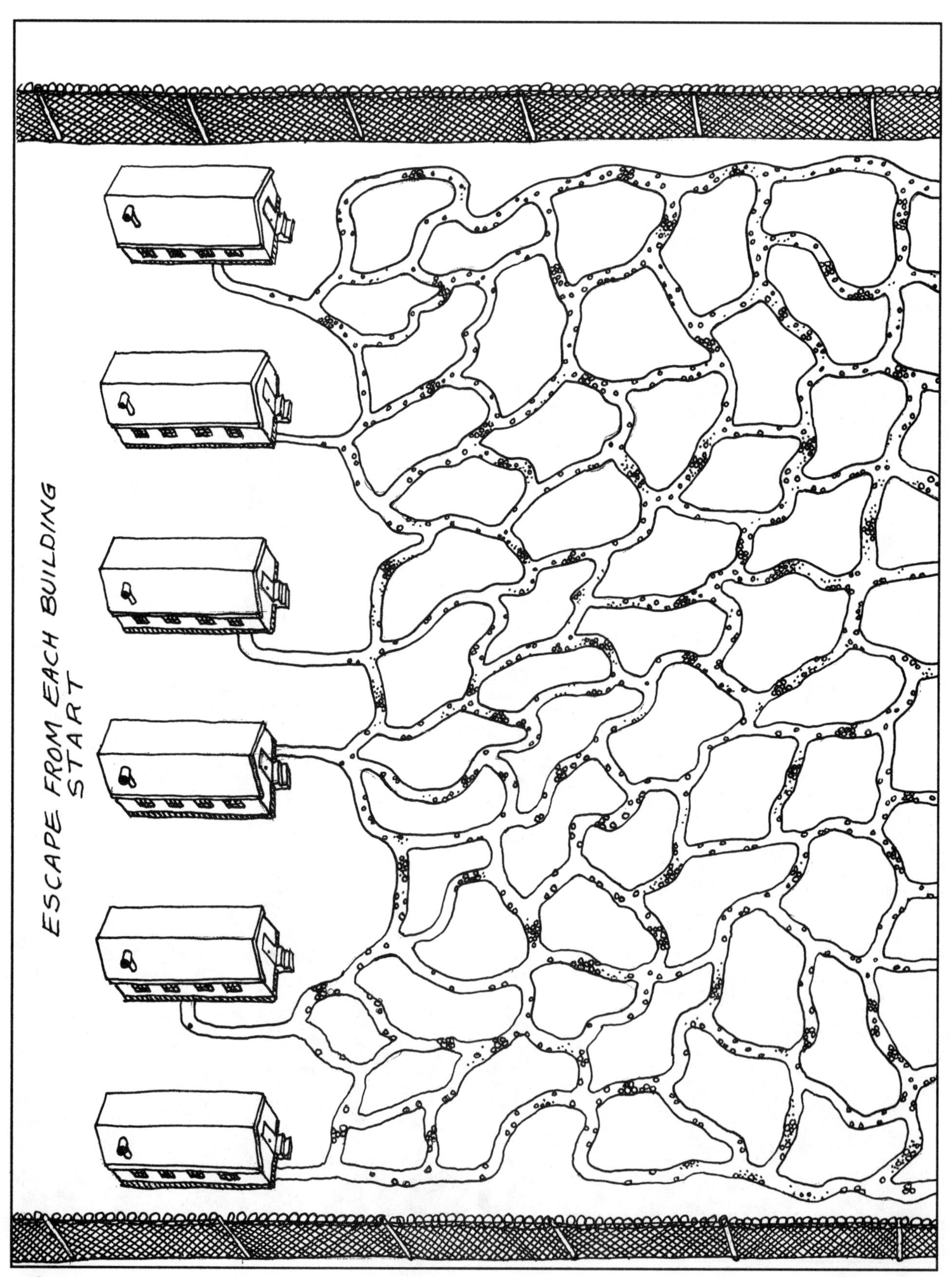

camp Stalag Luft III. For months, captured airmen dug several tunnels from their prisoners' barracks to the outside beyond the fence. Help the men escape from each building by finding a clear tunnel passage.

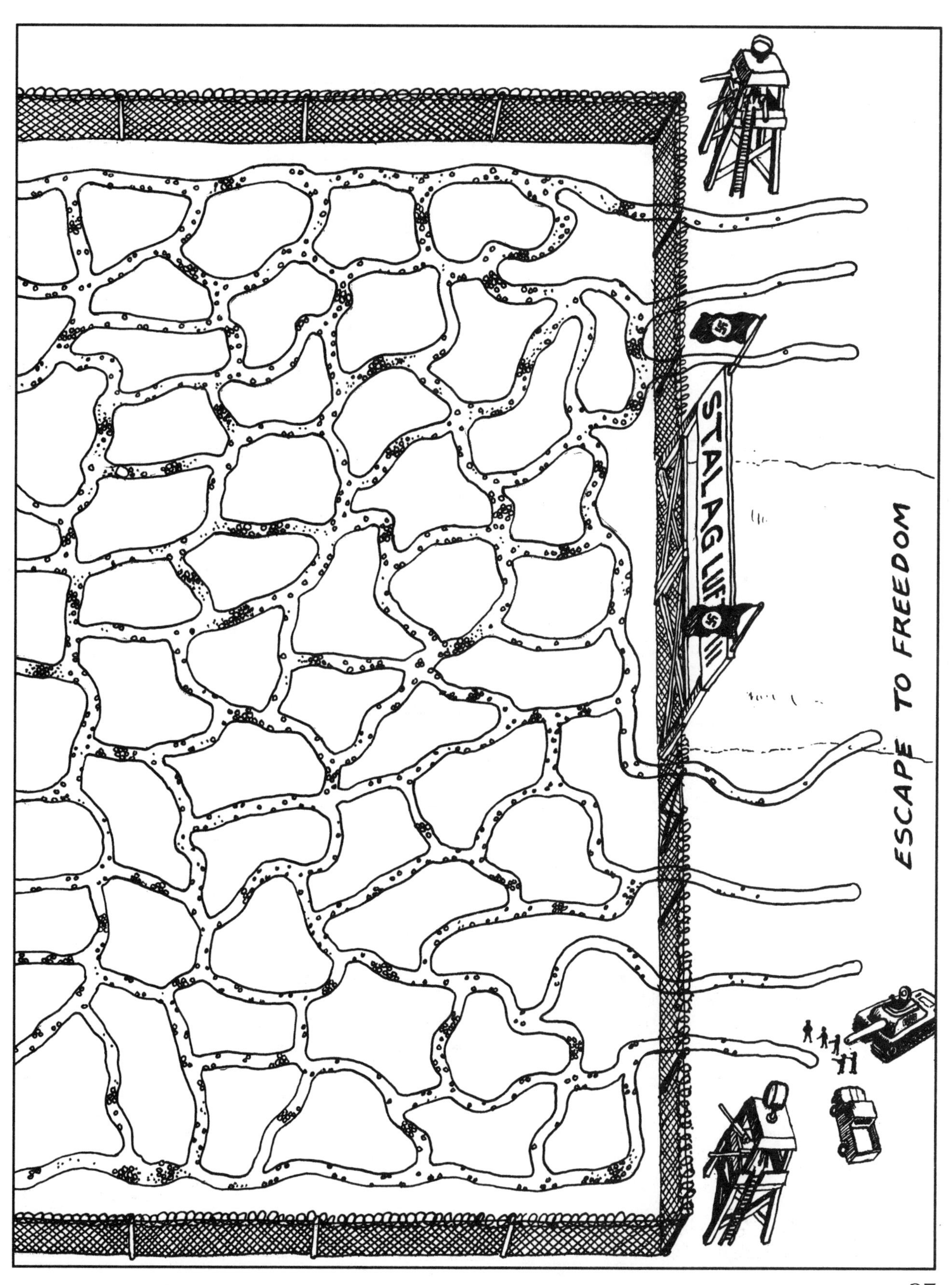

MacArthur Must Flee Corregidor

In 1942, the invading Japanese were advancing on Corregidor, an island fortress

off the Bataan Peninsula at the entrance to Manila Bay. It was important to get General Douglas MacArthur safely to the southern Philippines on a PT boat. Help the boat find a safe course through the dangerous currents.

Escape Under the Ocean

During World War II, many submarines had to escape terrifying enemy attacks.

This submarine has just made a successful torpedo attack and is trying to get away. Help the sub find its way through the exploding depth charges and escape to safety.

Escape of the Dalai Lama

Chinese Communist troops are storming up the steps of the Dalai Lama's summer

palace in Lhasa. He must escape to set up a new Tibetan government in exile. Help him move up and down the ropes and along the paths to freedom.

Escape from Alcatraz

Because of strong currents around the prison at Alcatraz Island in San Francisco

Bay, it has always been believed that no one could ever escape. Some tried and were never heard from again. Did they succeed? Put it to the test. Can you escape by swimming to shore?

Escape from Devil's Island

In French Guiana, in South America, there is an island prison known as Devil's

Island. You might be able to get away from this escape-proof island if you reached the coast and jumped into the sea. There you could attempt to swim to freedom. Find a clear path to the coast.

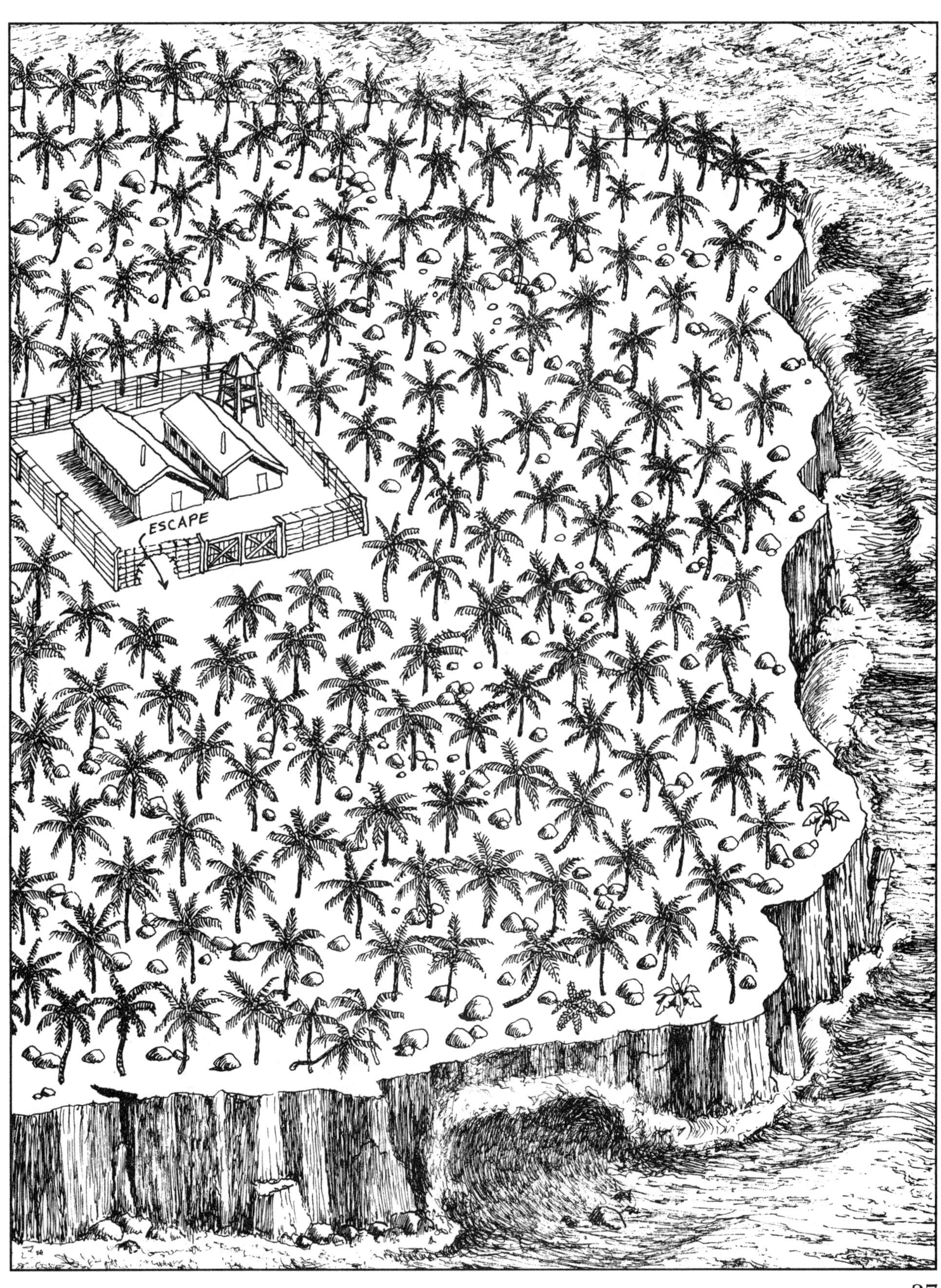

CONGRATULATIONS

The men who actually lived through these escapes and rescues experienced a lot. There is no doubt about that. You've had the opportunity to follow them in all of their escapes, and even though your efforts were not physically demanding and did not carry the same risks, you still had to muster up the determination and courage to face and complete each situation. You never quit or gave up, even though the going might have been tough at times. Chances are, as a product of your experiences with these great escapes, you will be better prepared to make your escape should that circumstance ever occur.

Great Escape Guides

If you had any trouble with the mazes in this section or would like to check your work, refer to the following guides for their solutions.

Crash of the *Italia*

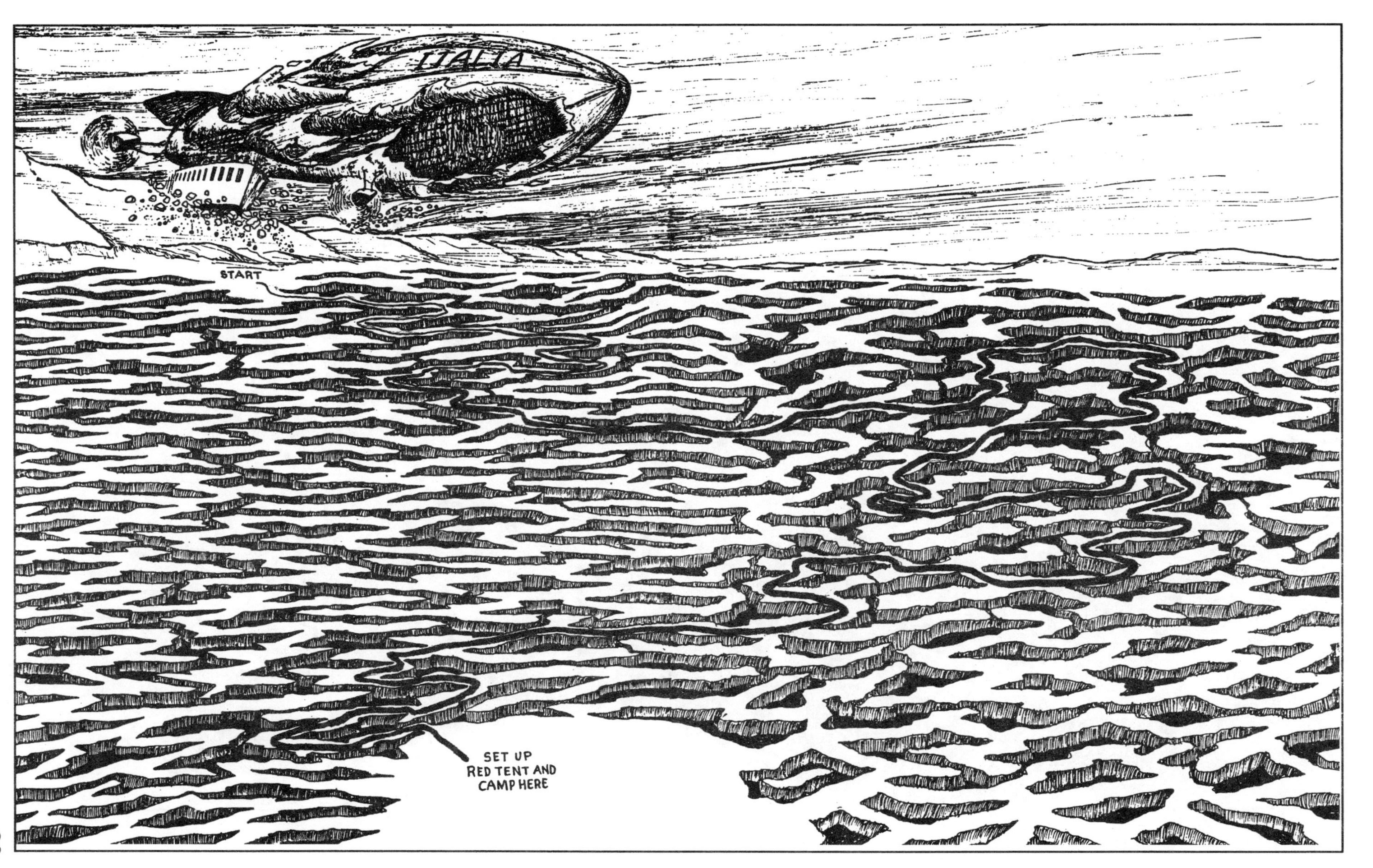

Search for the Red Tent

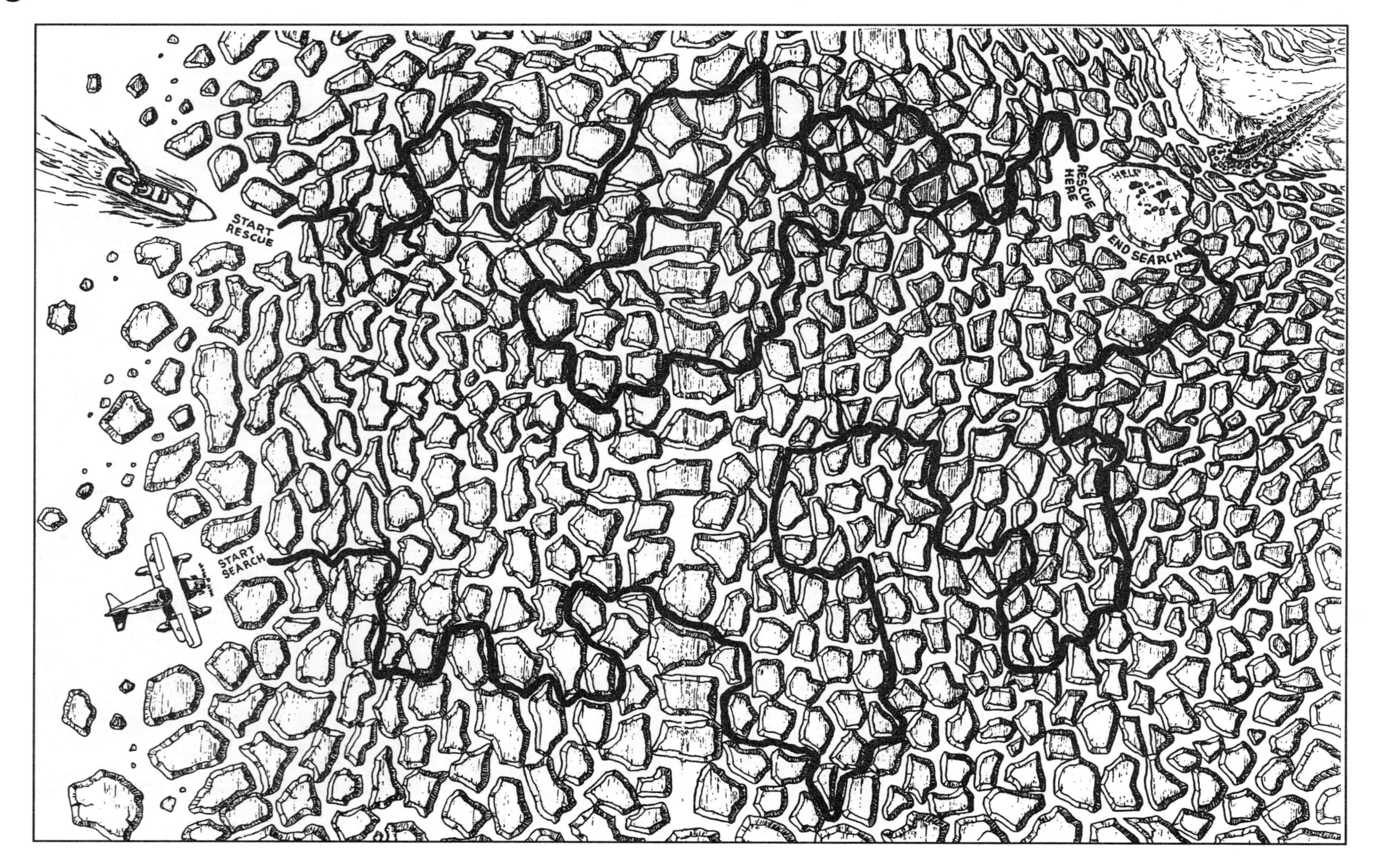

The *Hindenburg* Explodes

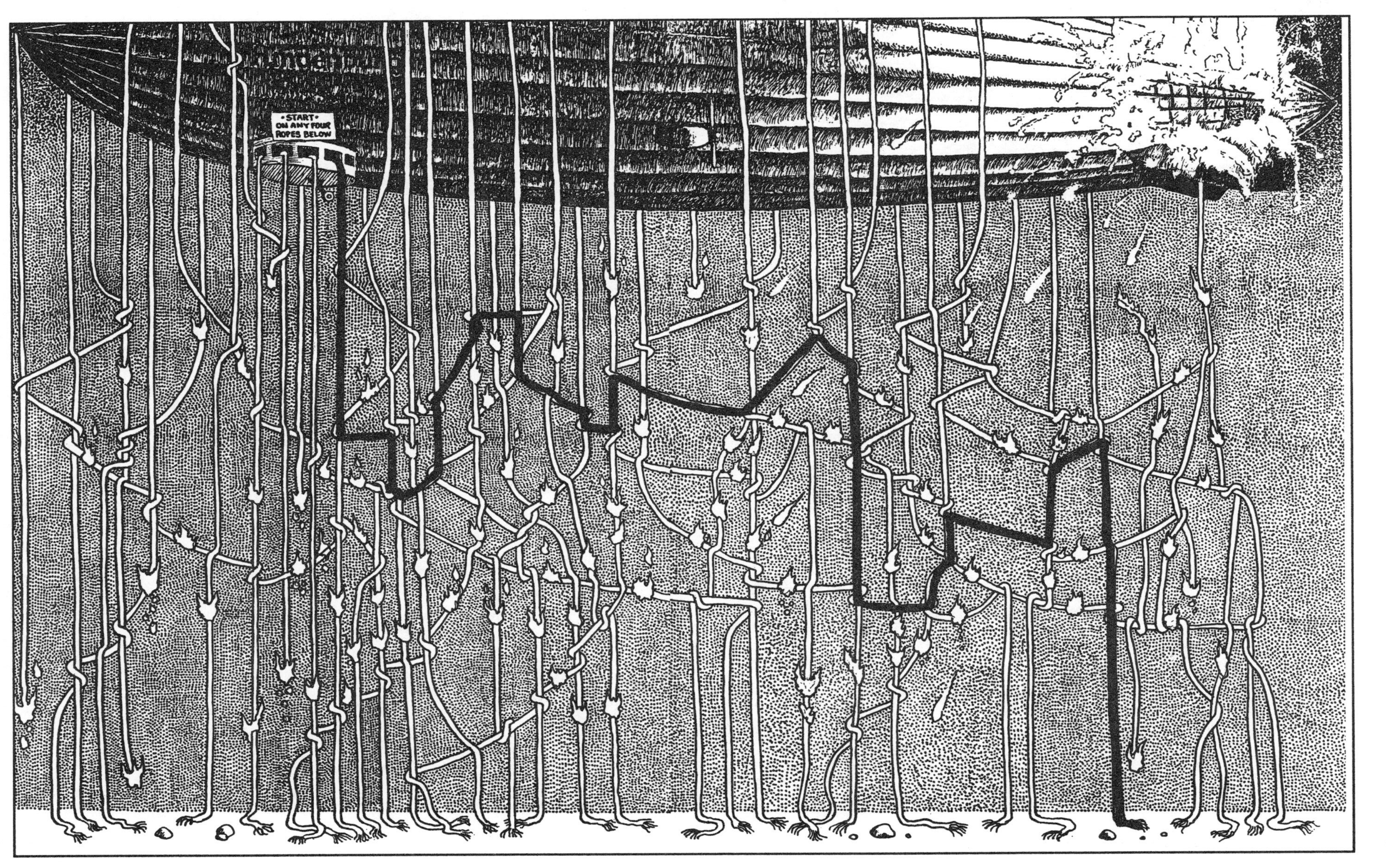

The *Squalus* Is Down

"Houston, We Have a Problem"

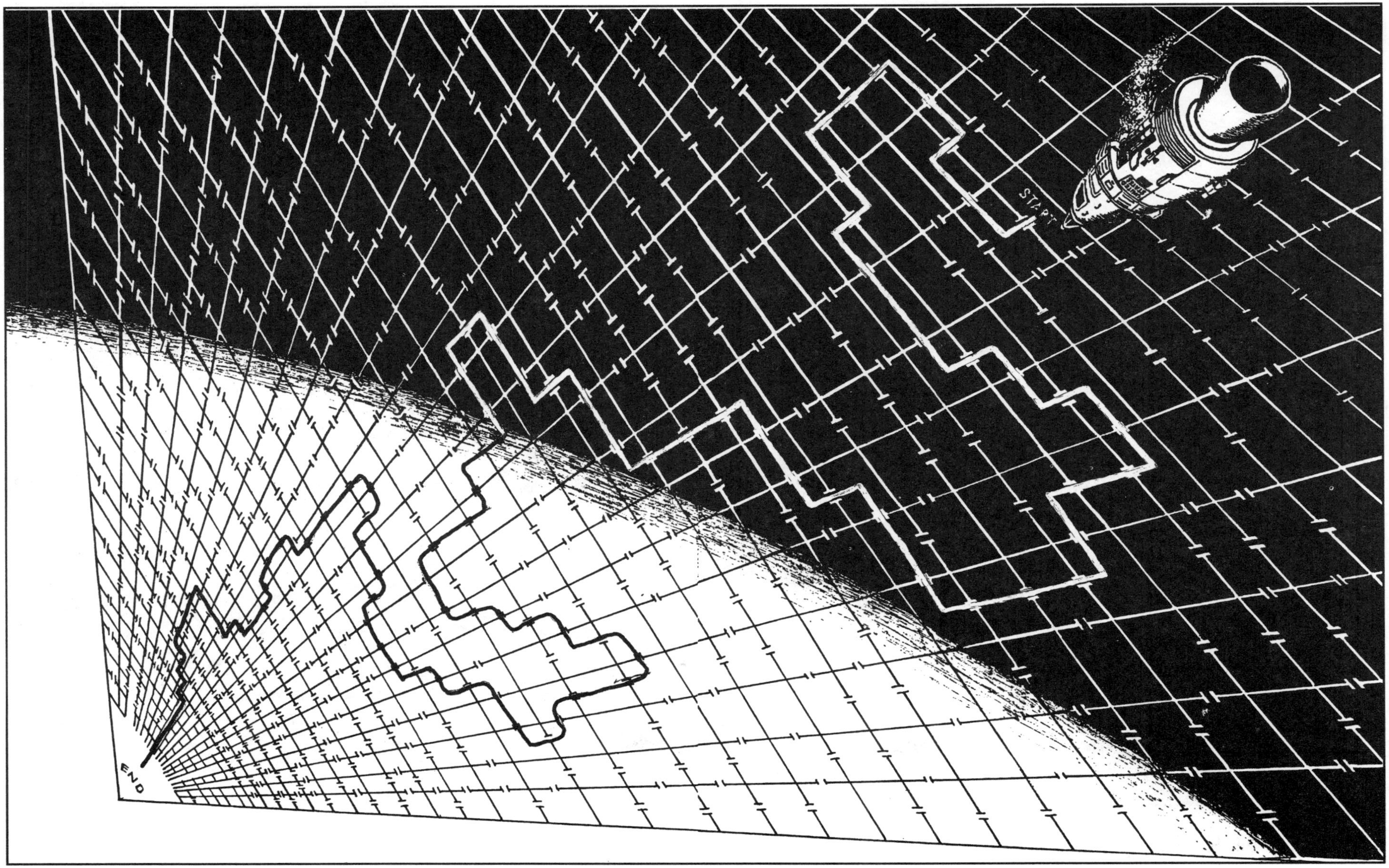

START

END

Crash in the Andes

Escape from Dunkirk

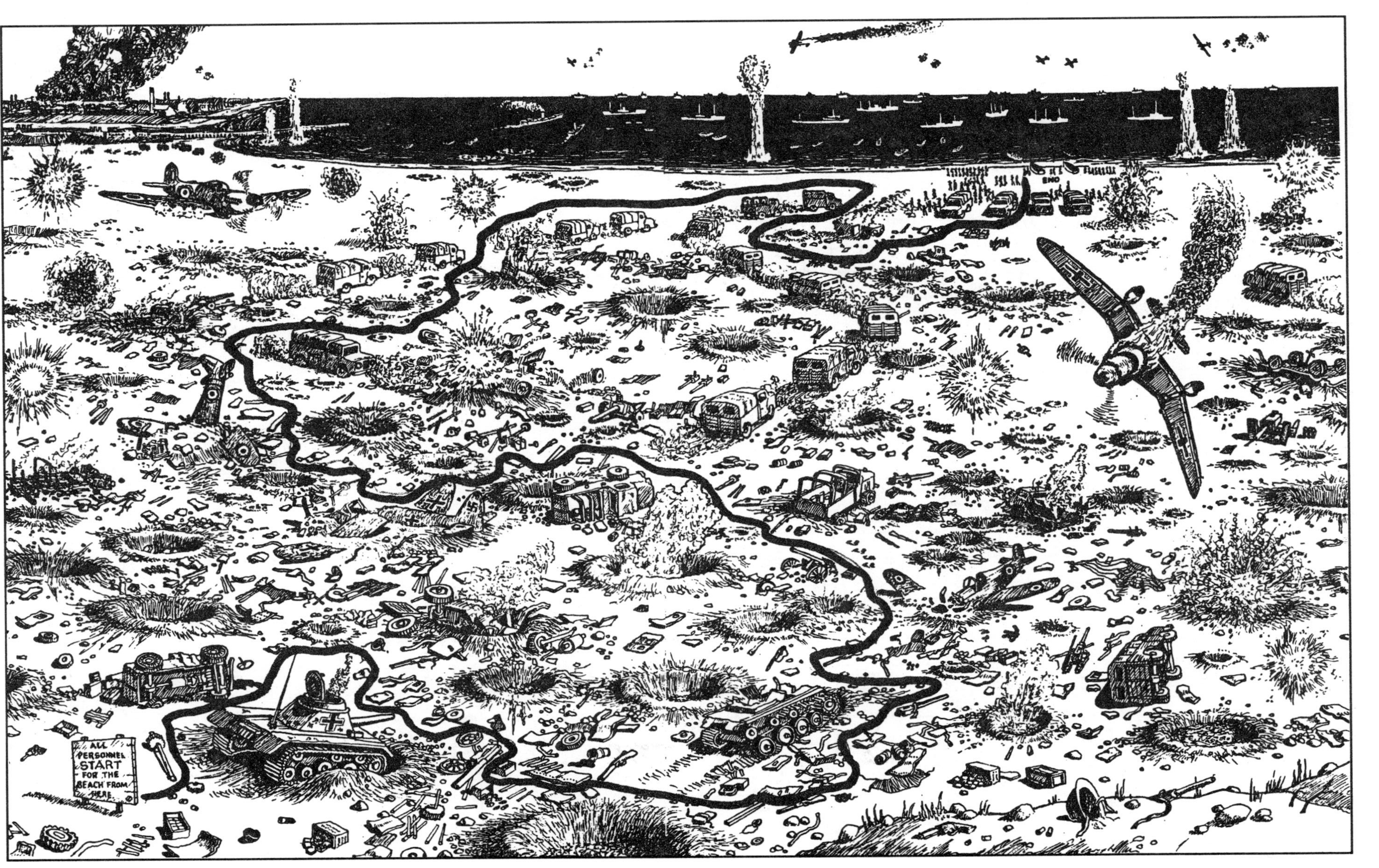

We Must Sink the *Bismarck*

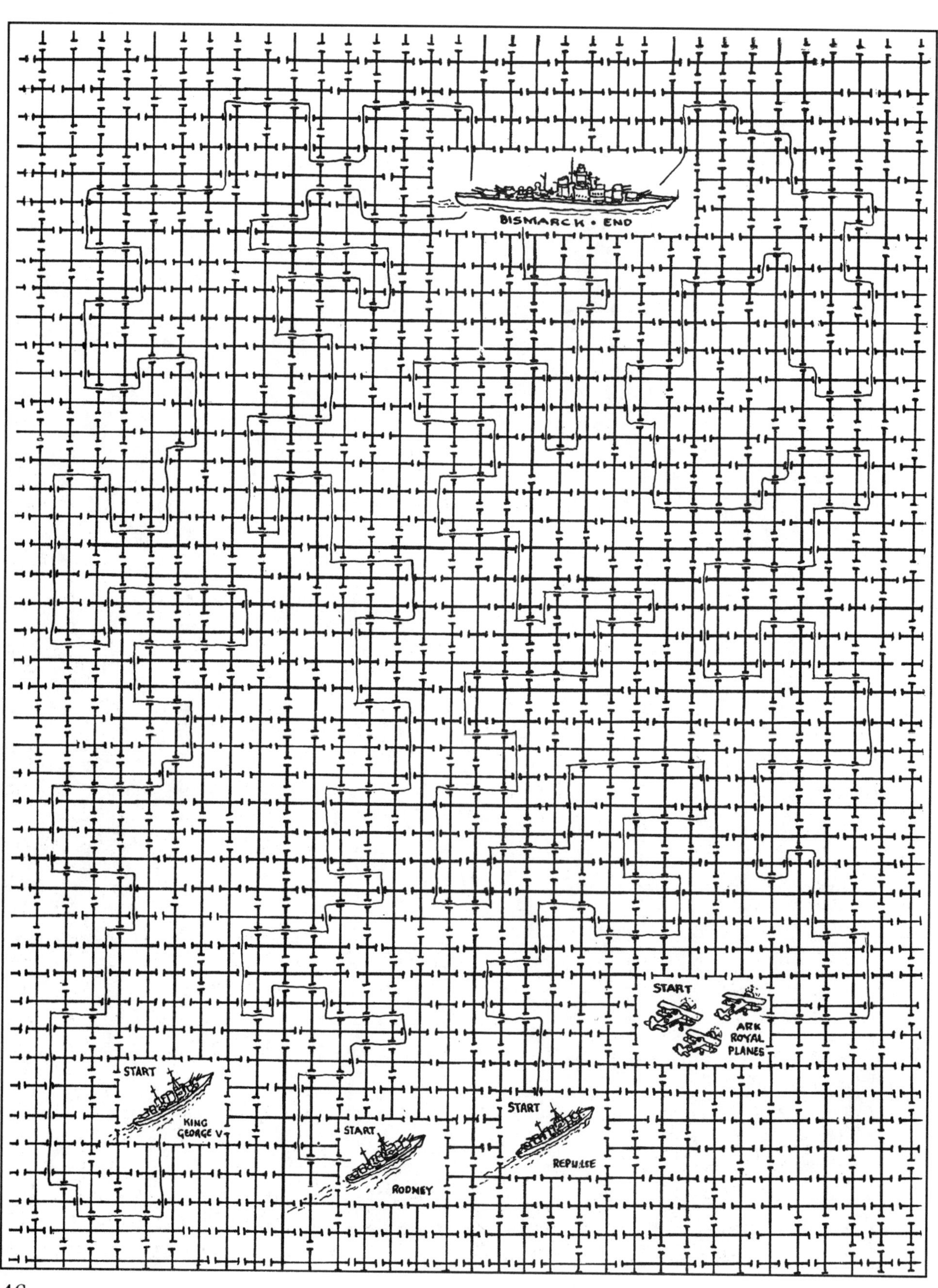

Doolittle's Raiders Down Behind Enemy Lines

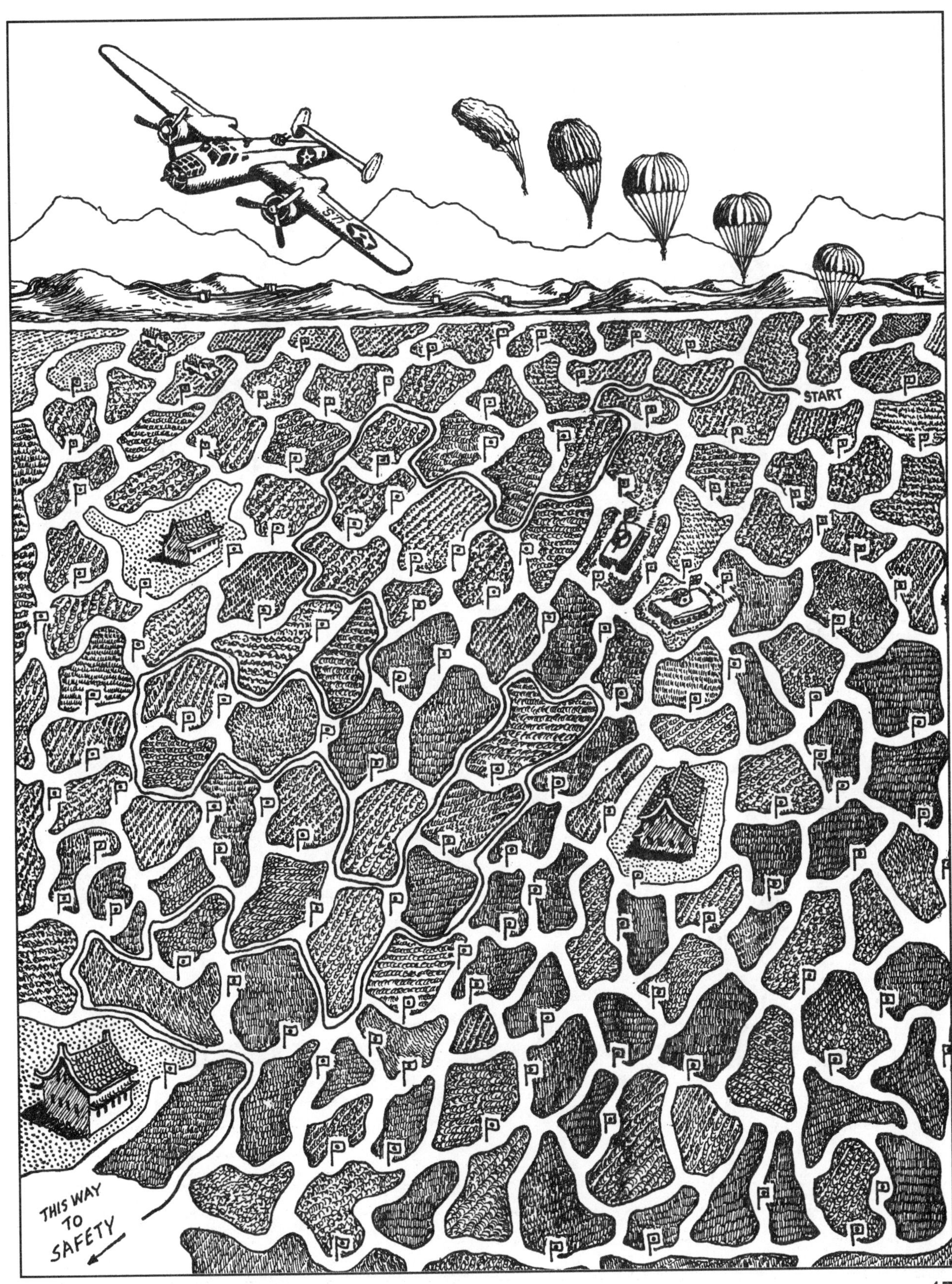

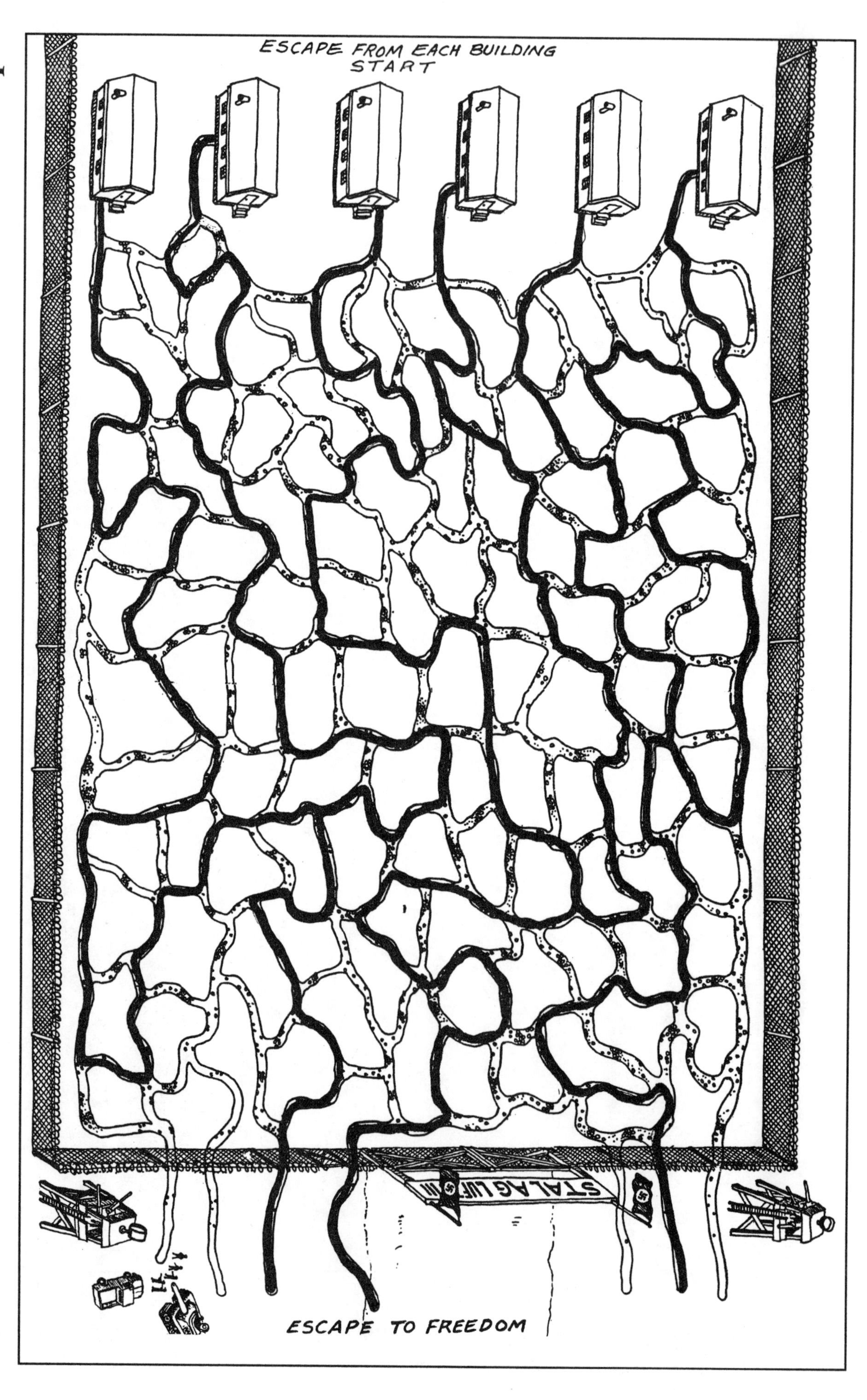
ESCAPE FROM EACH BUILDING
START
STALAG LUFT III
ESCAPE TO FREEDOM

MacArthur Must Flee Corregidor

Escape Under the Ocean

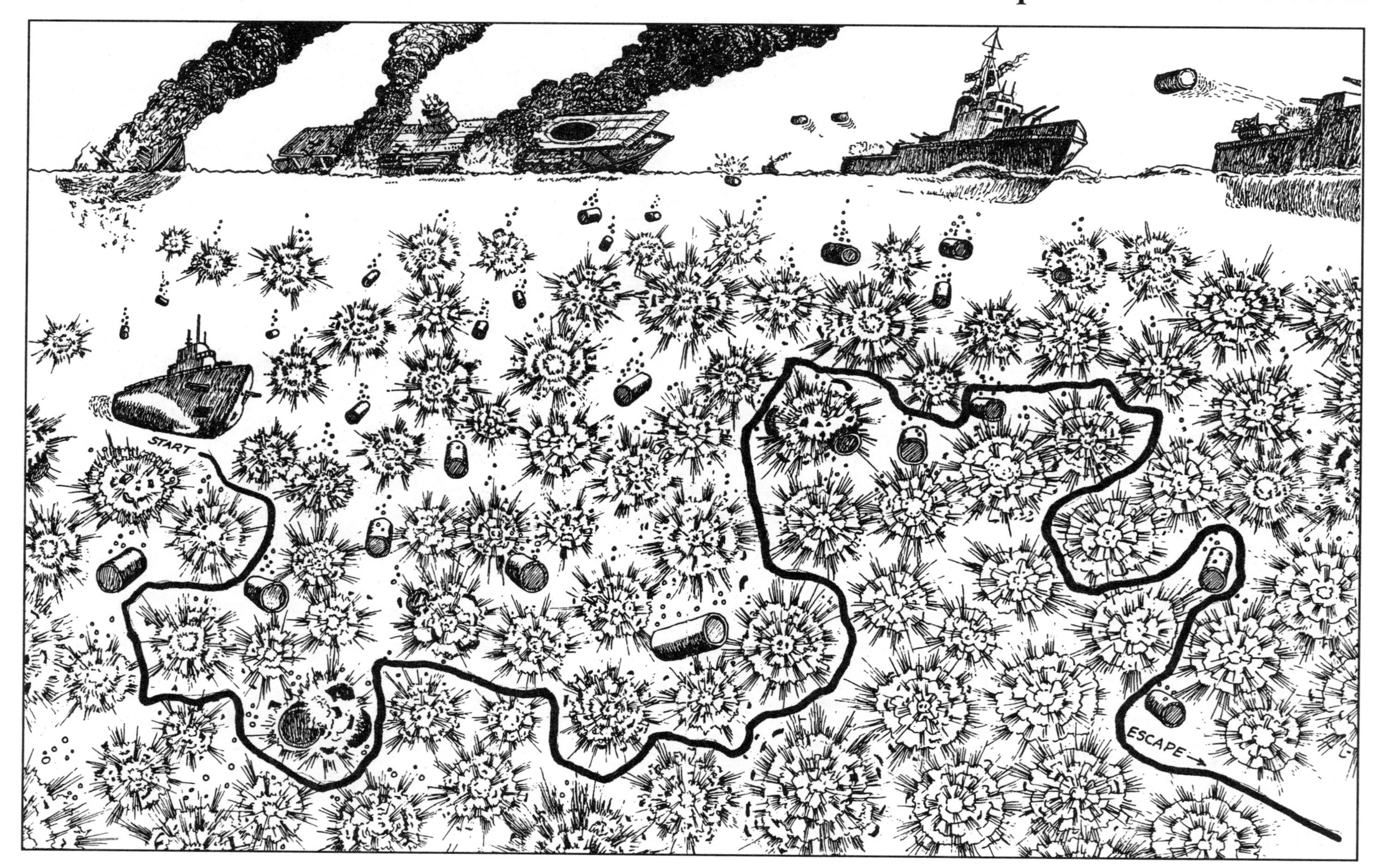

Escape of the Dalai Lama

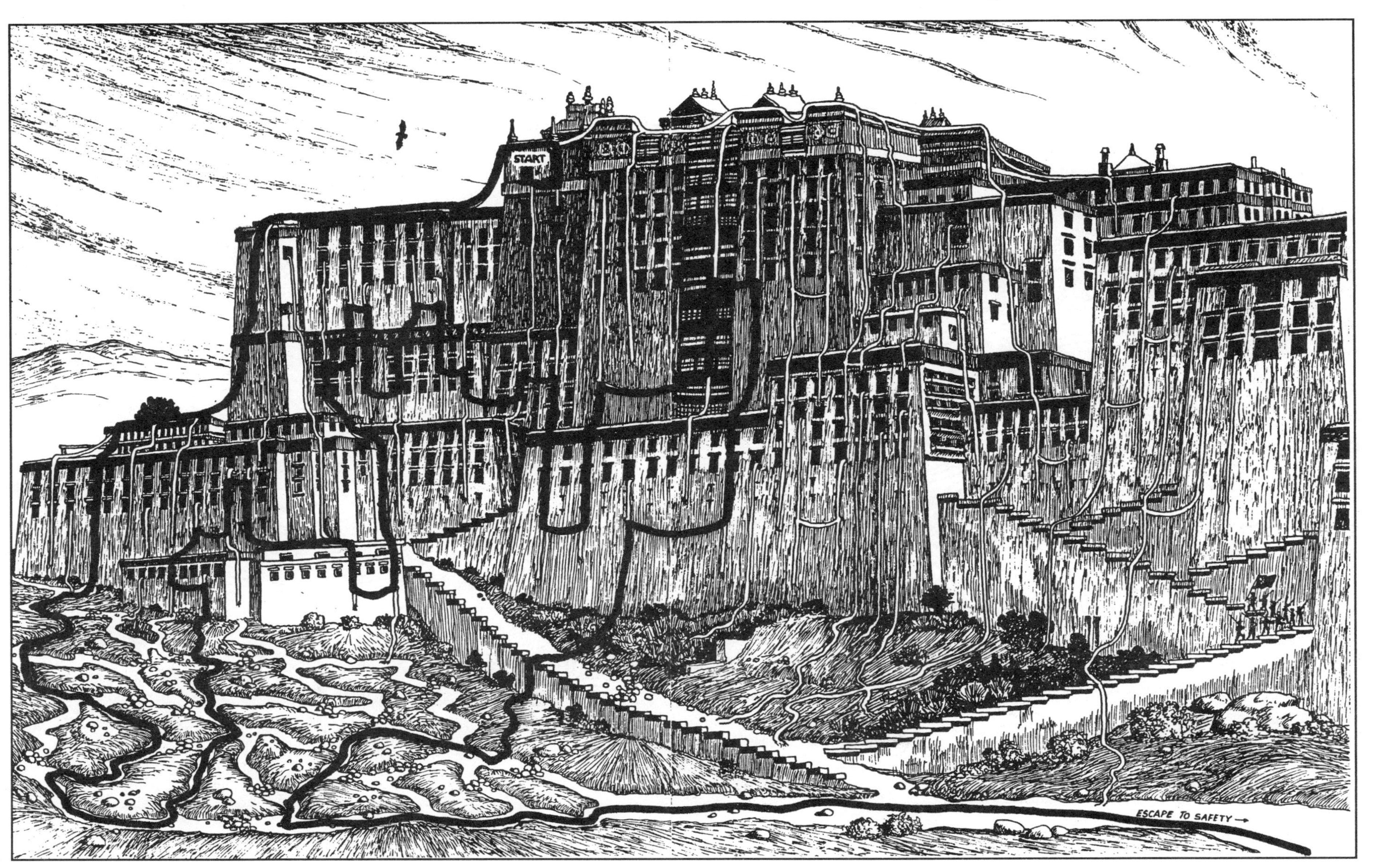

Escape from Alcatraz

Escape from Devil's Island

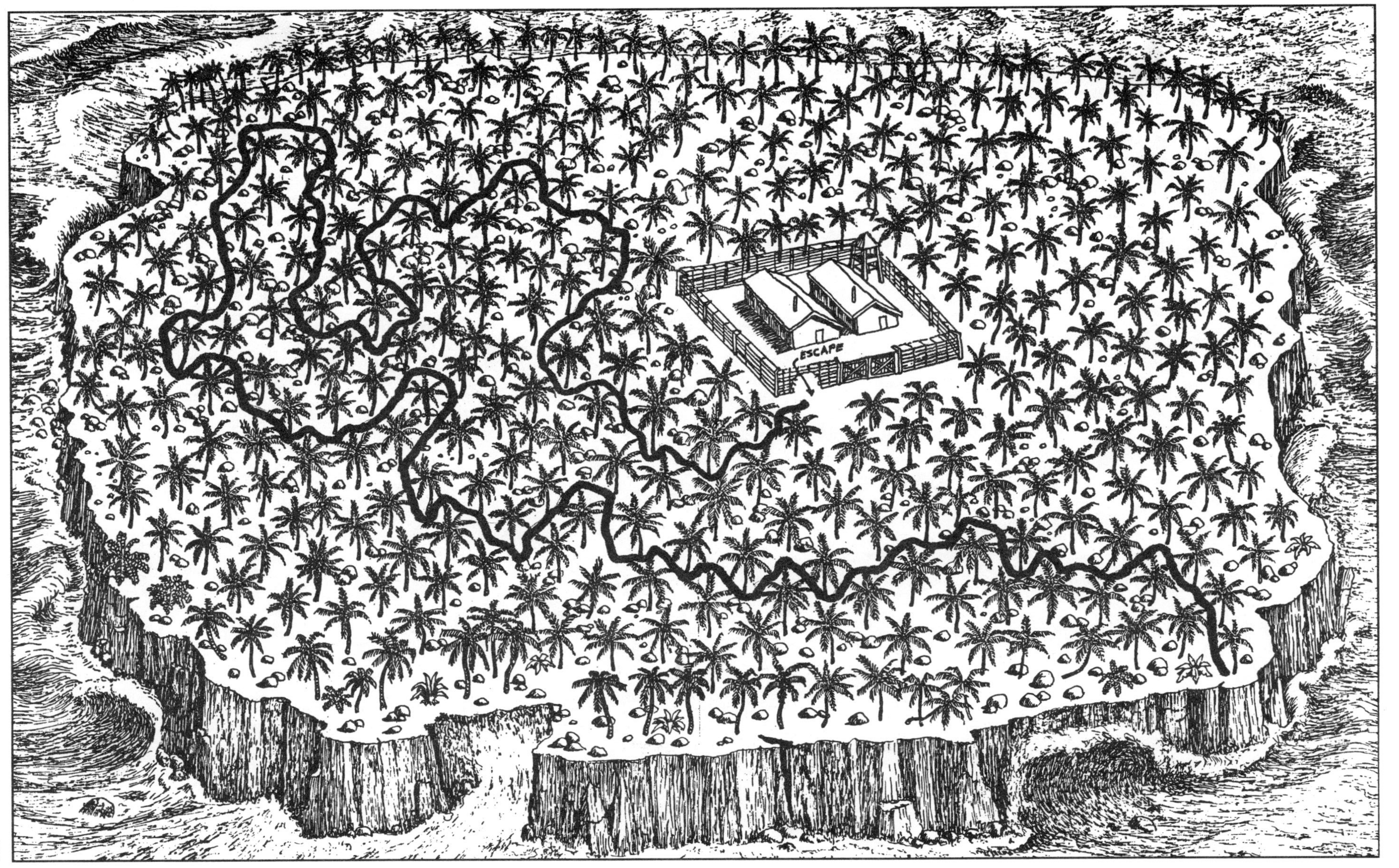

NATURAL DISASTER MAZES

CONTENTS

Introduction

We live on a restless planet. It heats up and cools down. Its atmosphere is usually calm and pleasant, but at times it can become extremely angry, with winds reaching hurricane force. Its surface appears to be asleep, but can awake with a sudden jolt so violent that it can reduce a city to rubble in an instant. It can belch out gases, rocks, and ash with devastating results that can affect the conditions on the planet for years to come. All of these events can bring terror to the hearts of the people and threaten their lives.

When changes that occur as natural processes in the planet's evolution become destructive, they are referred to as natural disasters. We have almost no ability to change or alter them. The best that scientists can do is warn us of an impending disaster so that we can find safety and try to save as much of our possessions as possible. Often, we will be lucky if we can just save ourselves.

Early warning is the key. That's where you come in. Many natural disasters are brewing on the following pages. People are in danger, but if they can be warned before the natural disaster occurs, lives can be saved. Your calling is to go forth and shout a message of warning. In many situations, you should have enough time, but in some cases where the disaster is in progress, you will have to hurry. You might have a tendency to want to turn back as you face the full fury of the disaster. Think of the lives you will save if you do not falter. Good luck.

Releasing Weather Balloons

These weather balloons are the best way to monitor the coming tornado. To release them, untie only the six ropes that are tied to them.

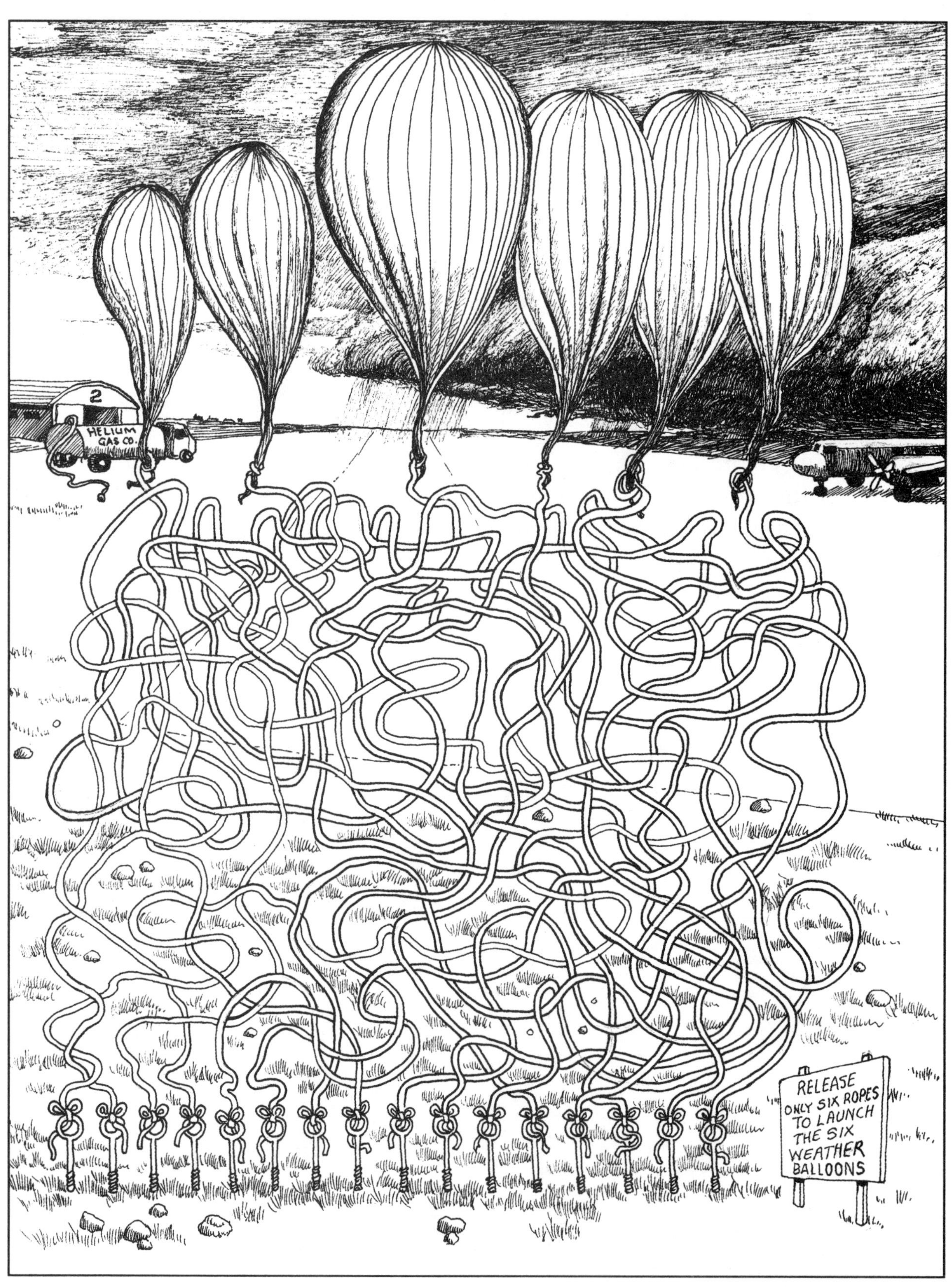

Tornado Warning I

Find a clear path through the cornfield to warn the town about the tornado.

Tornado Warning II

The tornado is fast approaching. Warn the people in this neighborhood by following a clear path and knocking on one door of each house. Do not backtrack.

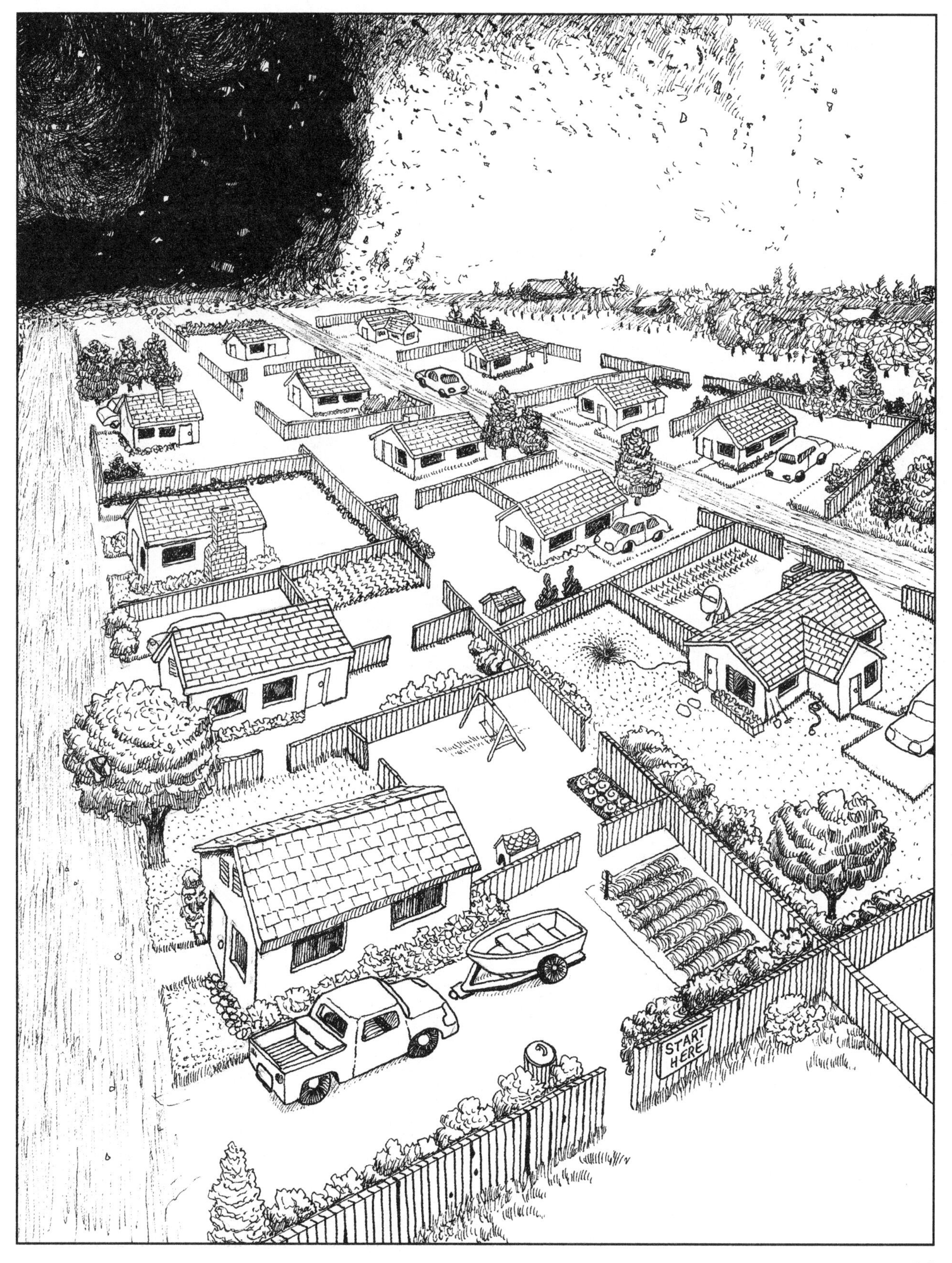
START
HERE

Escaping the Tornado

Drive to the storm cellar to escape the tornado! Do not pass any cars.

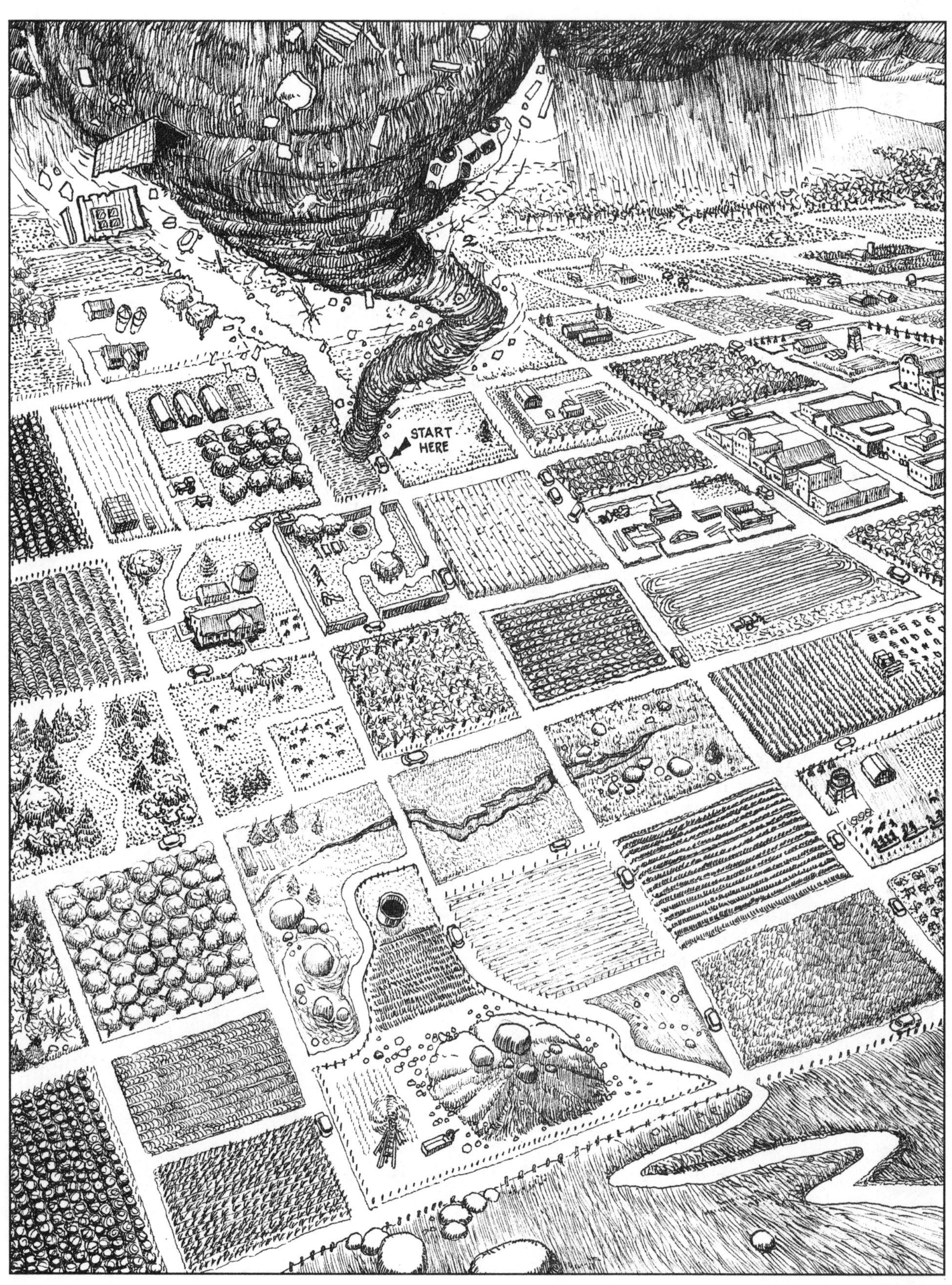

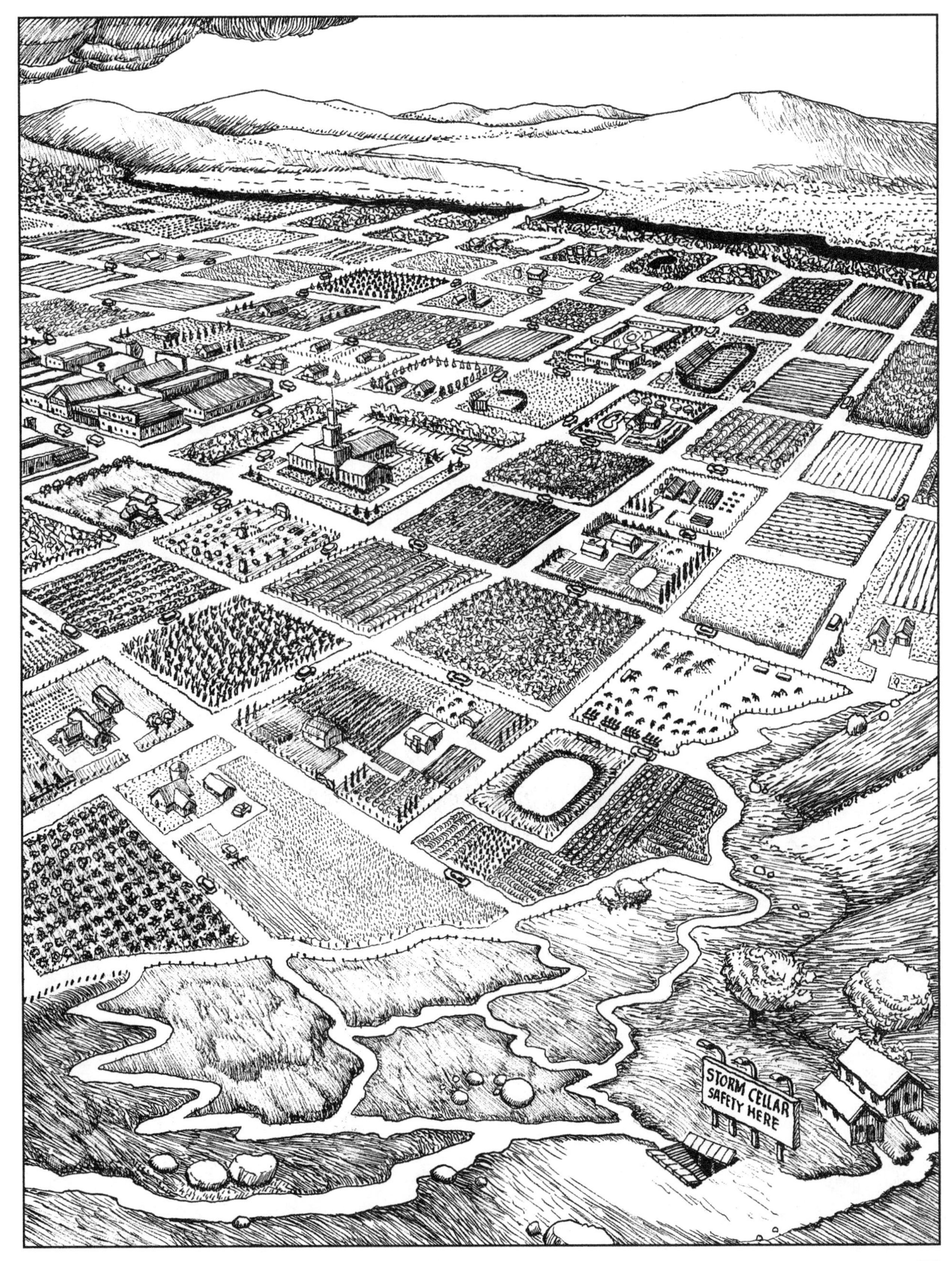
STORM CELLAR
SAFETY HERE

Finding the Hurricane's Center

To reach the hurricane's center, fly a clear path along the clouds.

Rescuing the Dog

To rescue the dog that has survived the hurricane, make your way on a path that winds past the debris.

END
HERE

Weather Satellite

To find your way to the weather satellite, you have to move through the openings in the grid the weather satellite has projected.

Strengthening the Levee

Make your way past these cow pens to the levee to strengthen it with sand bags before it breaks.

Saving the Animals

Save the animals that have climbed on top of the houses and barns by taking your boat to where each animal is located. Use a clear waterway. Don't backtrack.

END

Earthquake I

Find a clear path to the door of each building to warn the people of the earthquake.

HOTEL
STOP
HERE.

Shake, Rattle, and Roll

The earthquake is breaking up this freeway in a bad way. See if you can find your way off before it's too late.

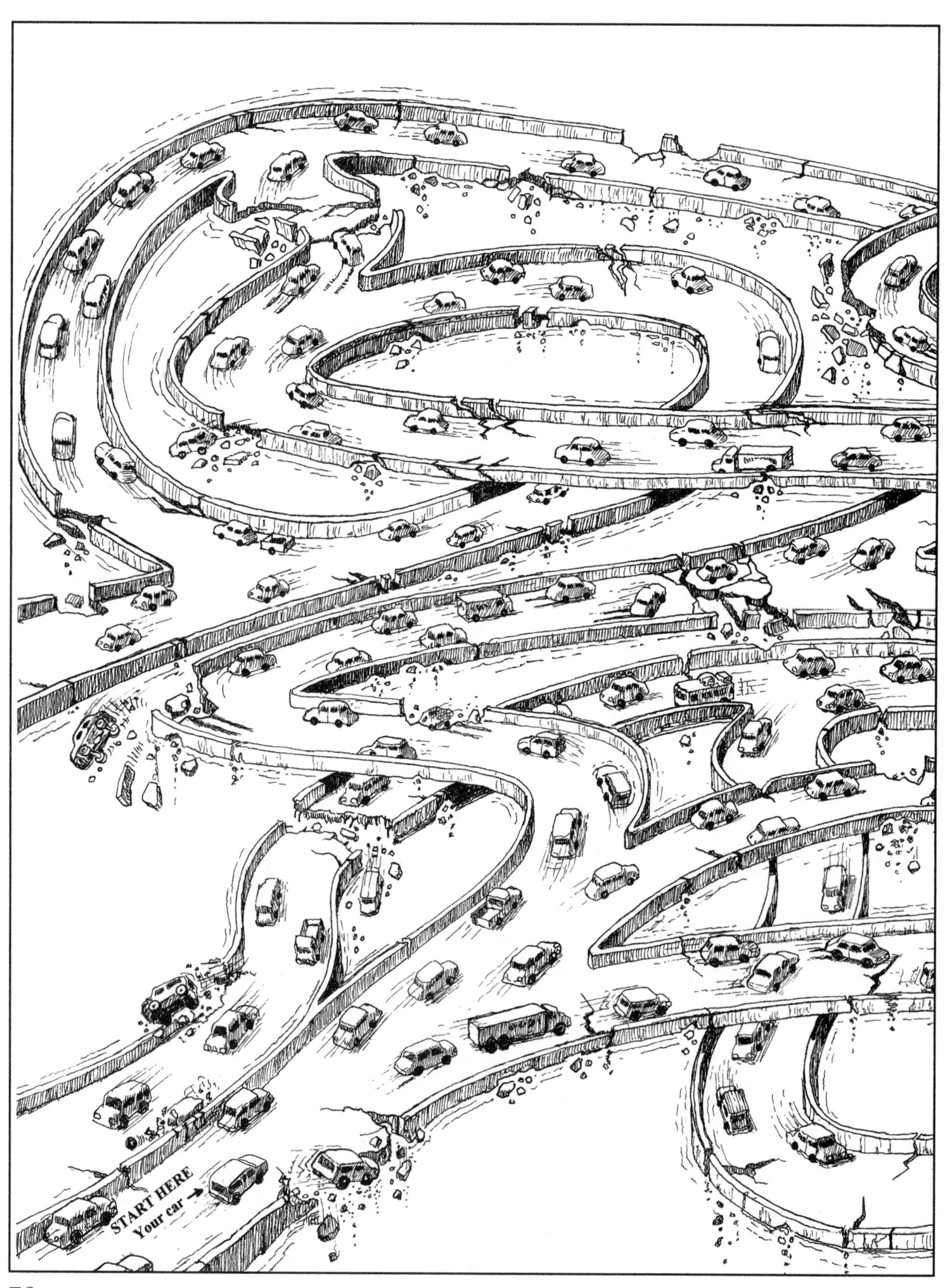

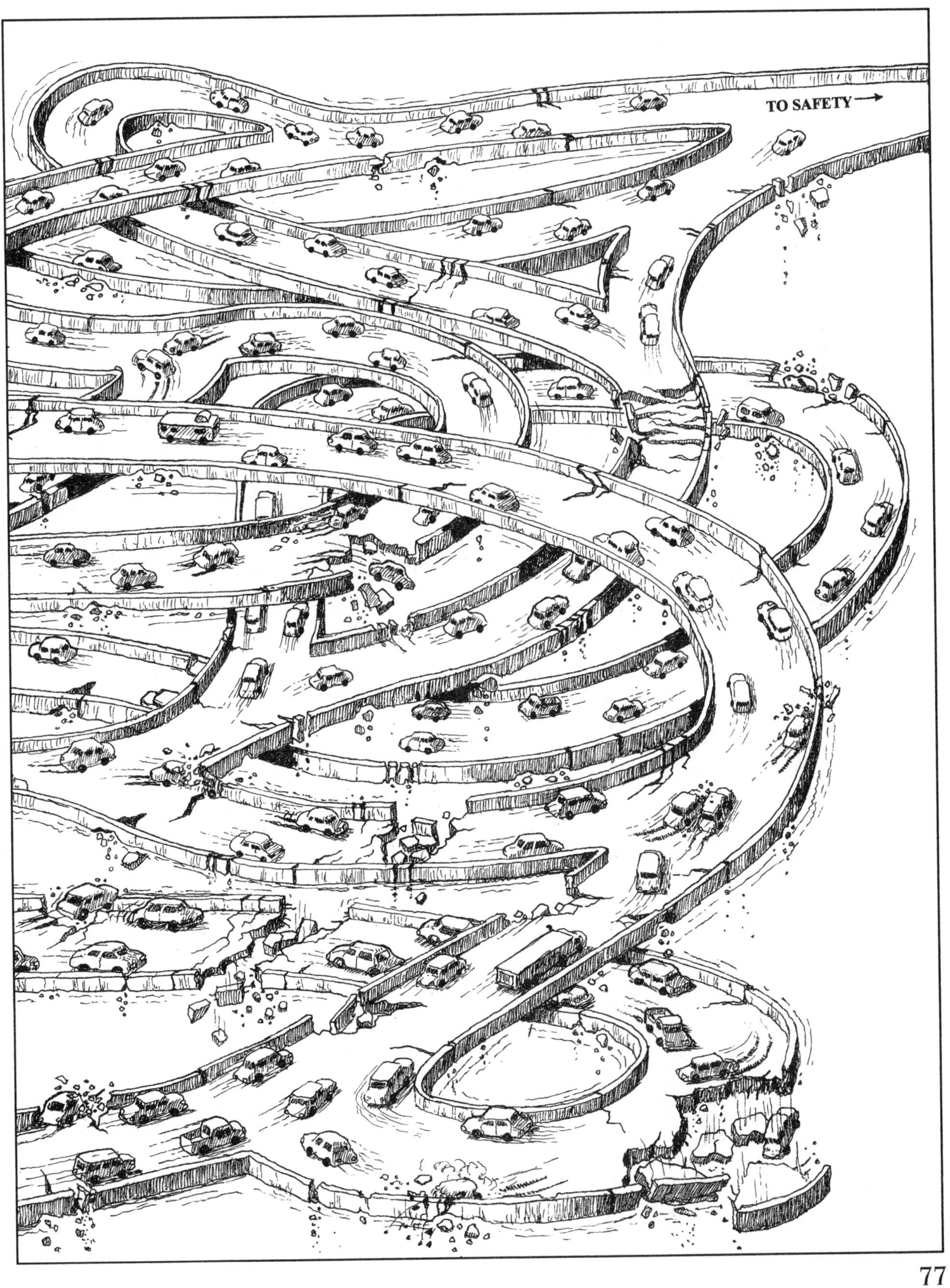
TO SAFETY →

Shut Off the Gas

One of the biggest dangers when an earthquake hits is broken gas lines. To turn

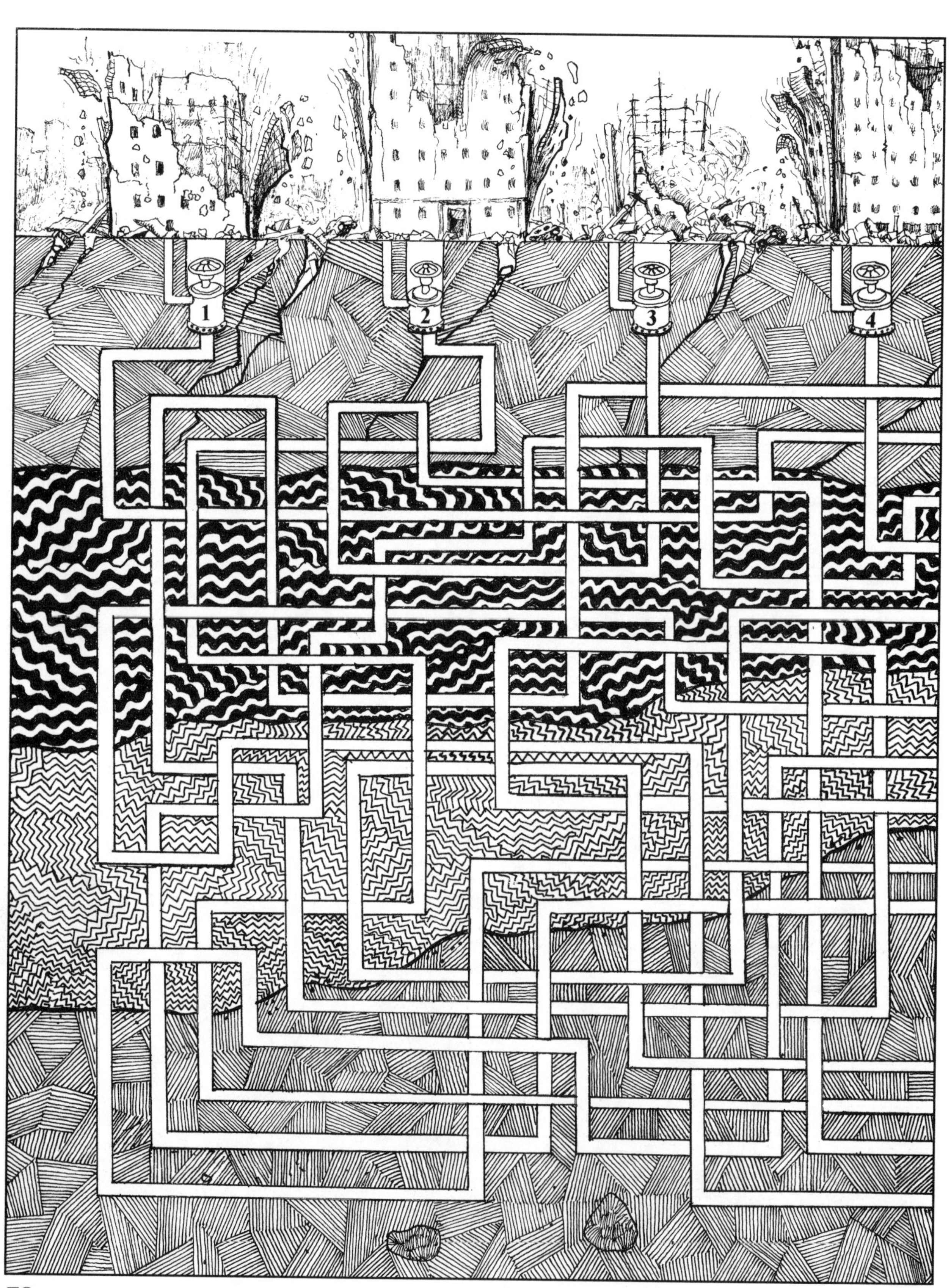

these gas lines off, you must do it in order one through seven. To do this, begin on the right and follow each line. Place the valve number on the unnumbered valve.

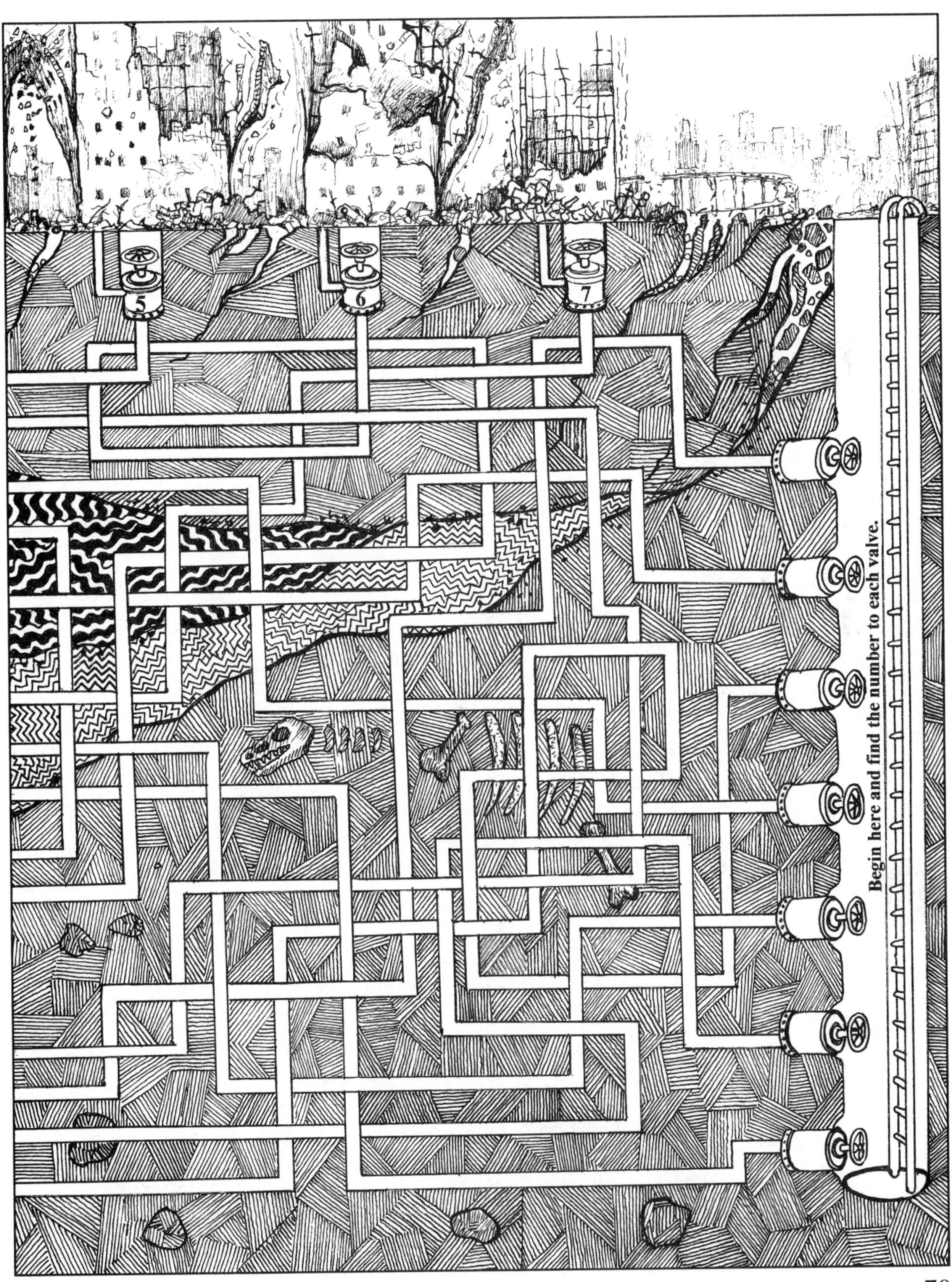

Demolished

The 1906 San Francisco earthquake demolished the city. It has happened again! Find a clear road across the city and escape.

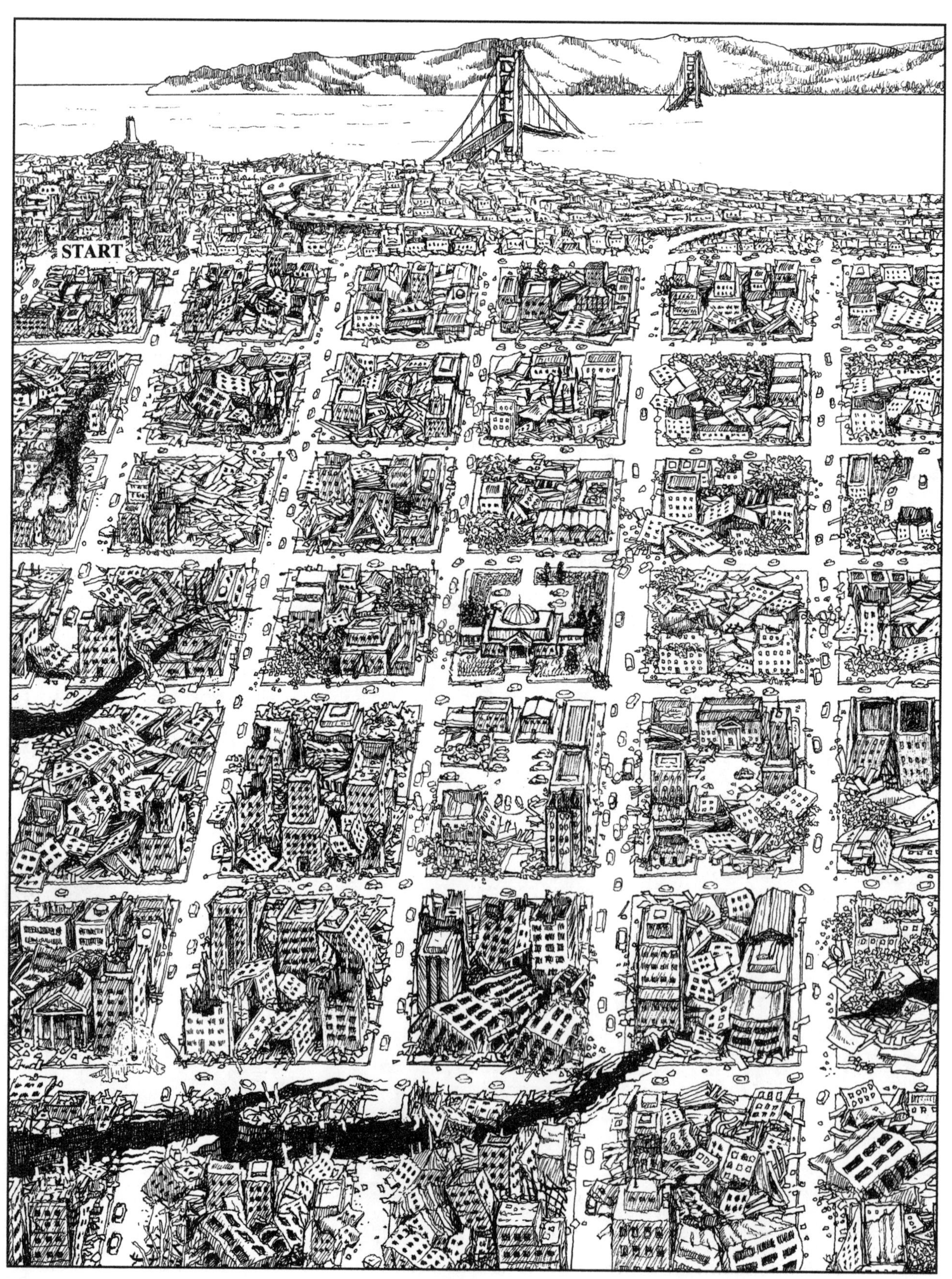

Earthquake Detection

There are many scientific instruments to monitor and measure earthquakes. The

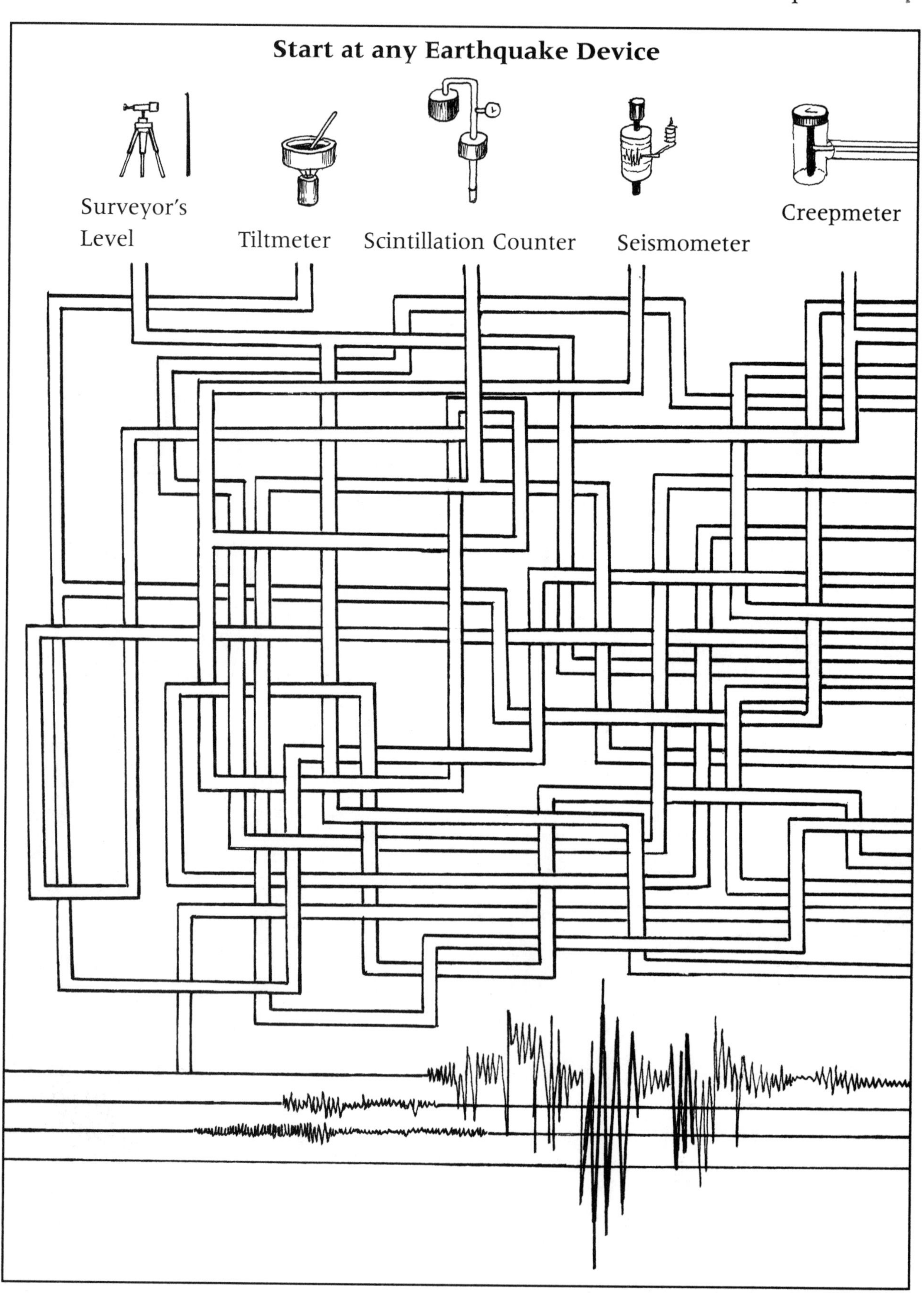

force of the San Francisco quake is indicated by the very jagged line below. Find out which instrument monitored the quake by following the instrument's connection to the line.

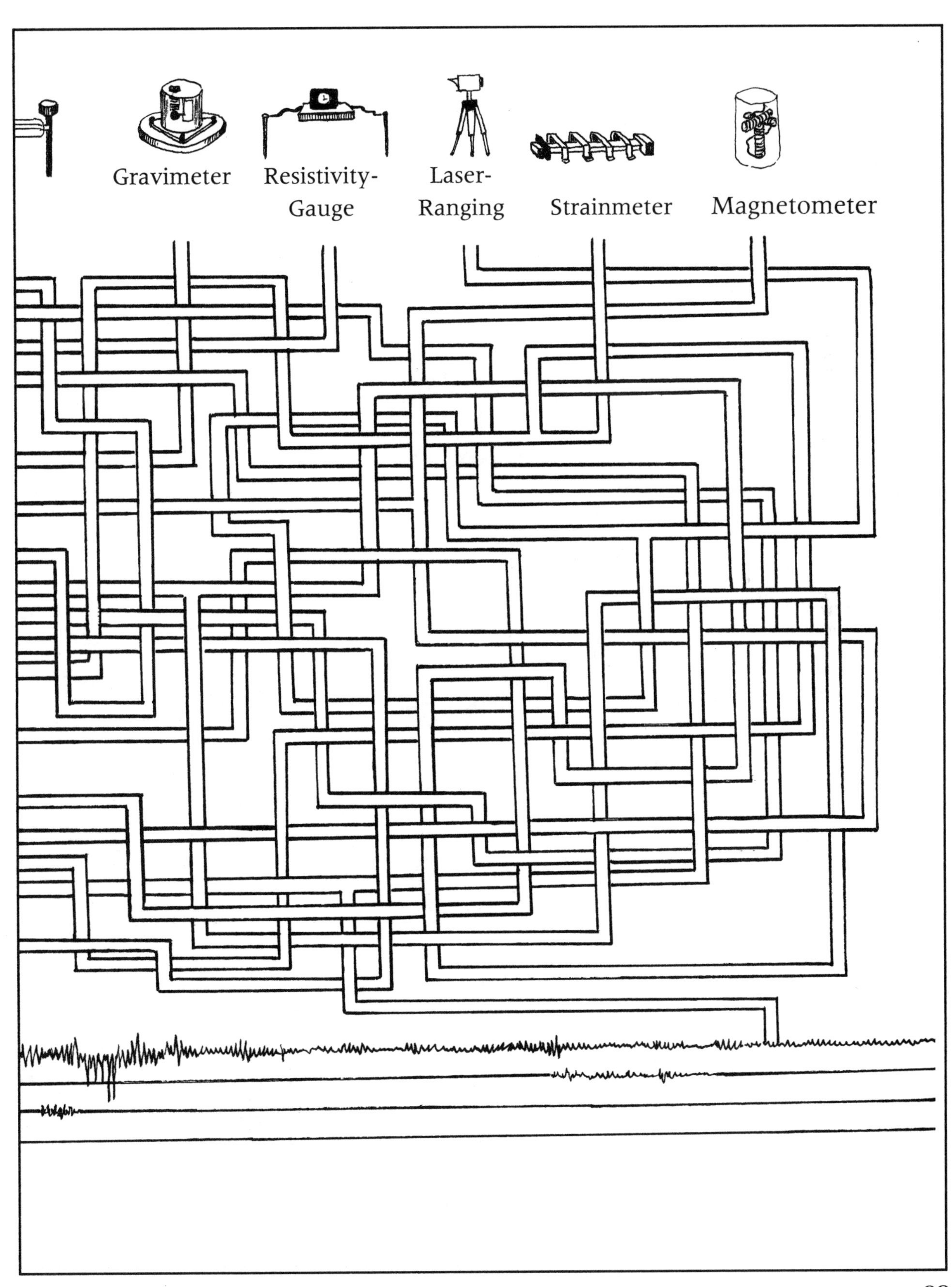

The Alaska Quake

On March 28, 1964, an 8.6 earthquake hit Anchorage, Alaska. It was devastating. See if anyone is injured in that car by finding a clear path to it.

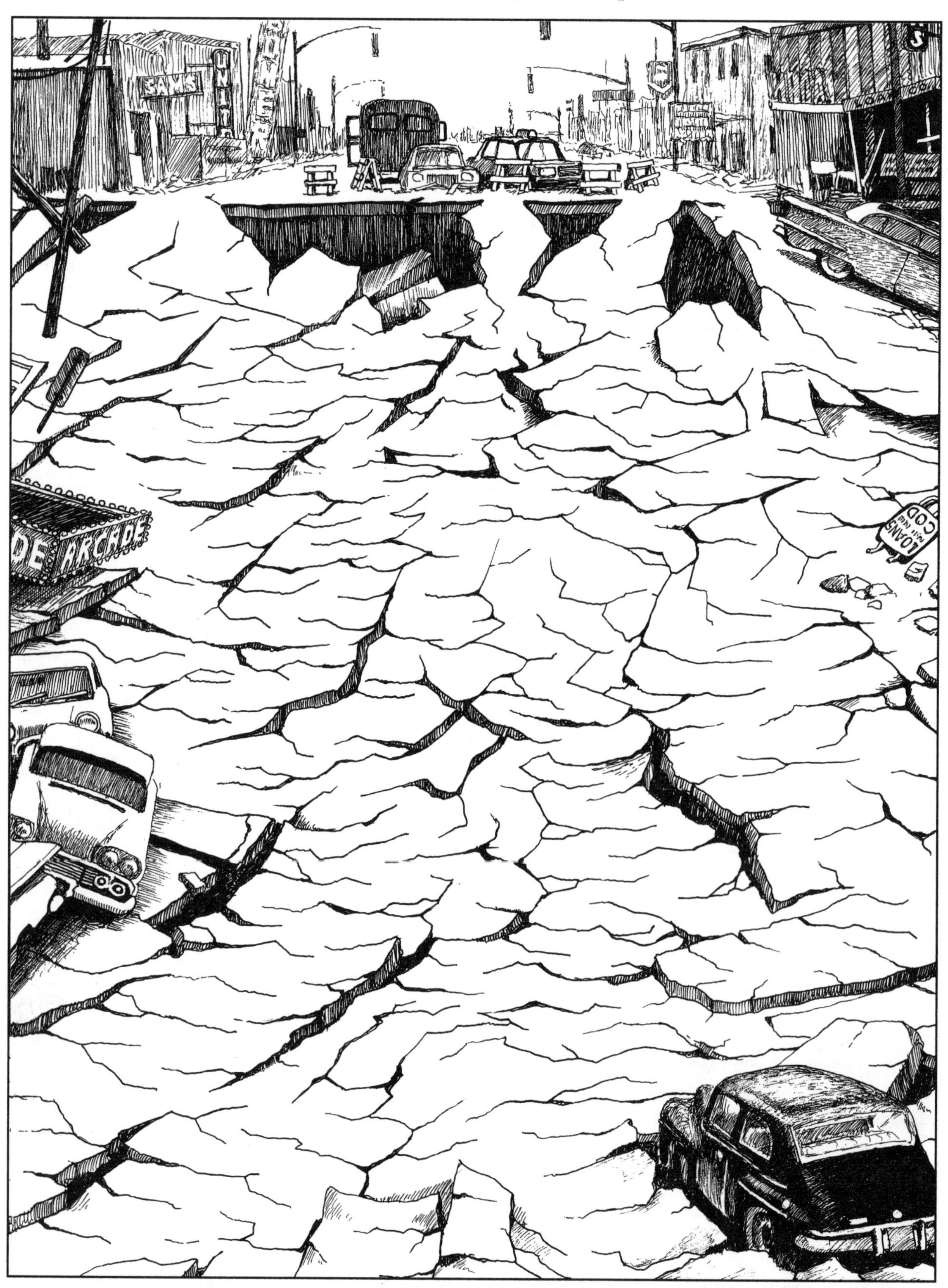

Help!

Help the family in this house find their way to the road by moving from ice block to connecting ice block.

Tsunami

A tsunami is a giant wave, or a tidal wave, that is caused by an earthquake. The

Alaska quake produced a tsunami that caused a lot of damage. Escape from this tsunami by cutting across the field ahead of the wave. Avoid the cracks.

The Ruins

Mexico suffers many earthquakes. Here lie the ruins of a small town as a result.

Make your way through the remains of the town to the church. Find a clear path, and hopefully the town's people will be there.

Tidal Wave

Work your way along the extended shoreline to warn the two people about the tidal wave. Then escape!

EXIT
HERE
FAST

Preventing an Avalanche

To prevent the potential avalanche, climb the mountain and place dynamite on the snow overhang. Stay off the rocks.

Avalanche I

Warn the vacationers of the impending avalanche by knocking on each window. You can move up the ladders and along the balconies, but do not backtrack.

Avalanche II

Your task is to save the skier and, finding a clear path through the trees, escape to the rock on the right.

FIND SAFETY
HERE

Yellowstone National Park Fire

These sleeping campers are in trouble! Rescue them from the fire and the stampeding buffalo by making your way to their tent and escaping.

Planting Trees

Plant a tree at each flag to reforest this burned-out area. Don't backtrack.

Placing Probes

To figure out when this volcano might explode, place two probes into the hot magma.

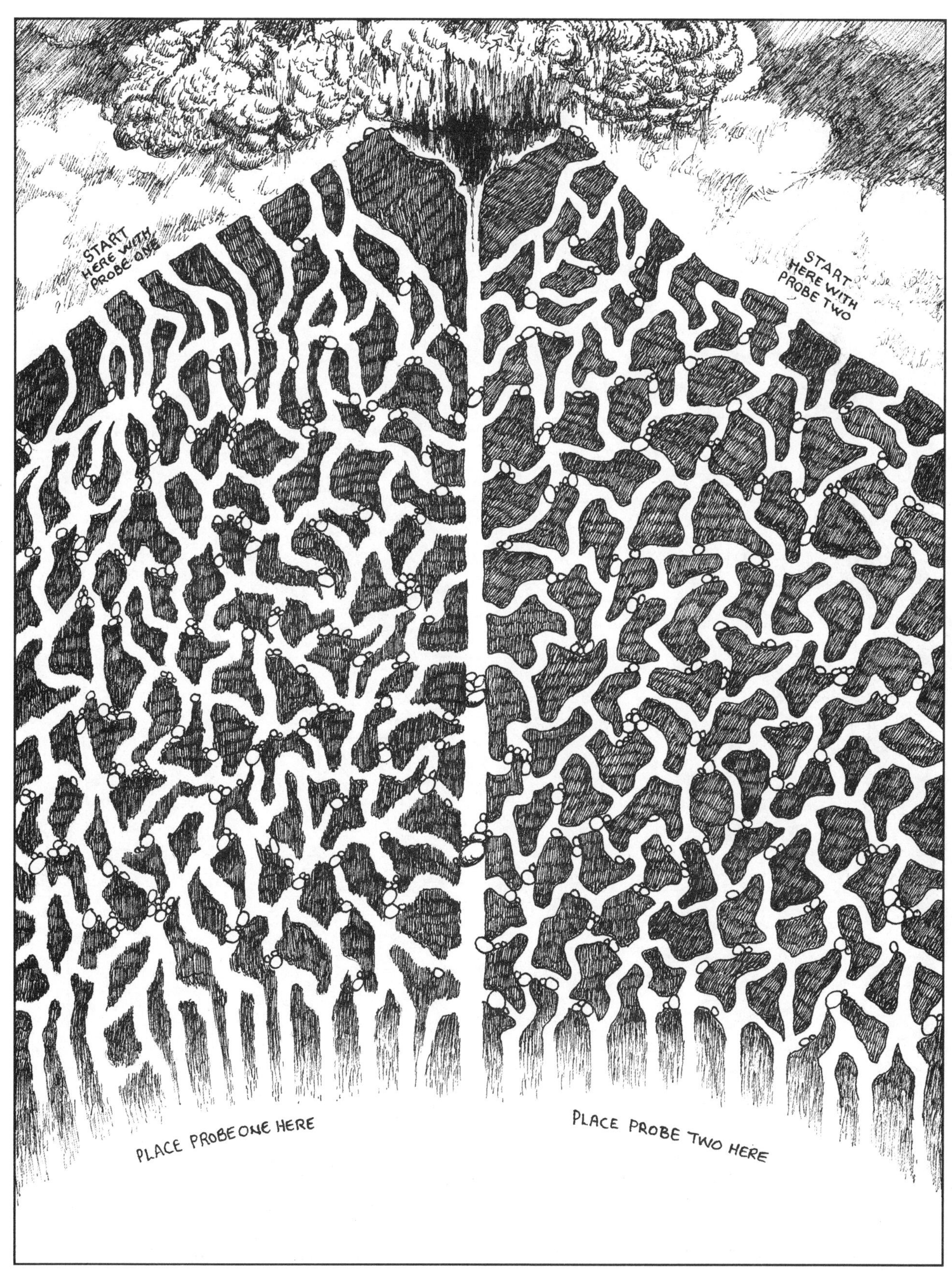

Placing a Sensor Probe

Find your way down the tunnels to place a sensor probe that predicts earthquakes. Avoid the rocks that block the tunnels.

It Could Go Anytime!

Get down as fast as you can!

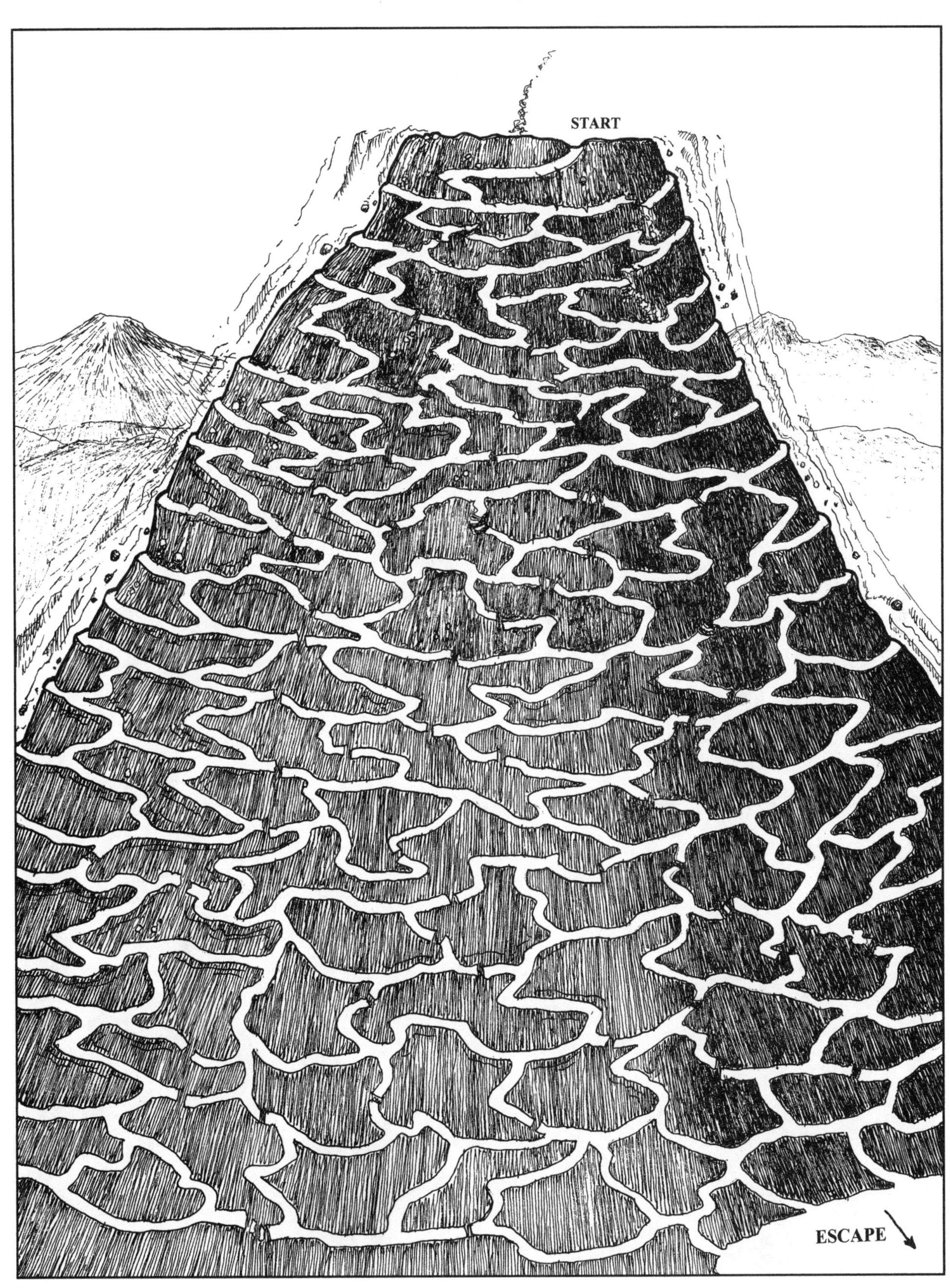

Volcano II

Your only escape from the slowly moving magma is to make your way over the trees that have fallen but not yet burned.

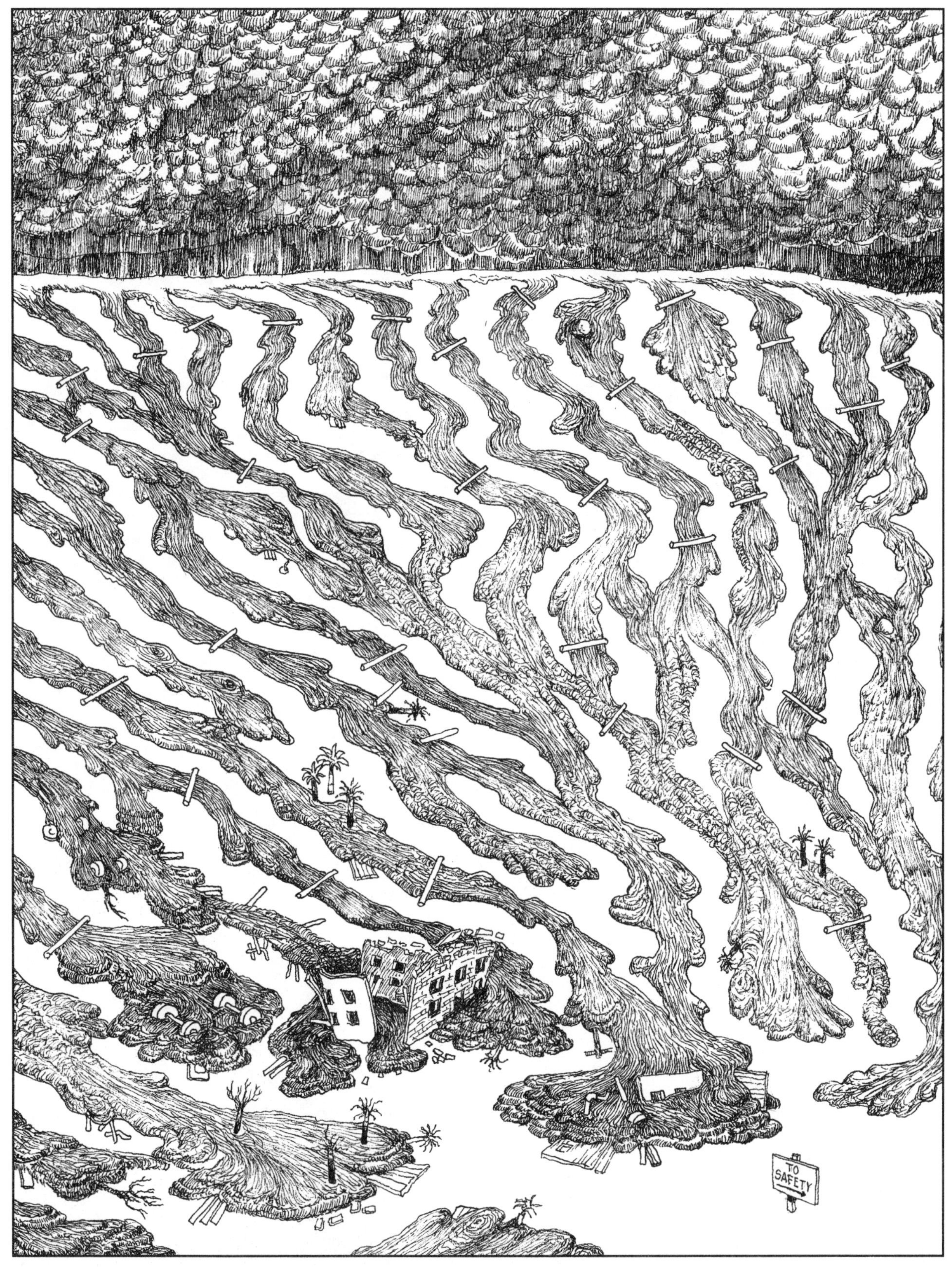
TO SAFETY

This Doesn't Look Good

Mexico has many volcanos. Towns are sometimes very close to these volcanos.

It looks like something big is about to happen, so get out of town fast by finding a clear path.

The Calm before the Eruption?

Observe this crater and then find a clear path to the waiting sports utility vehicle.

START
END

Mount Vesuvius

It is one o'clock in the afternoon, August 24, A.D. 79. Vesuvius is blasting forth with an eruption that will bury the city of Pompeii. Find a clear path through Pompeii and escape in the boat at the pier.

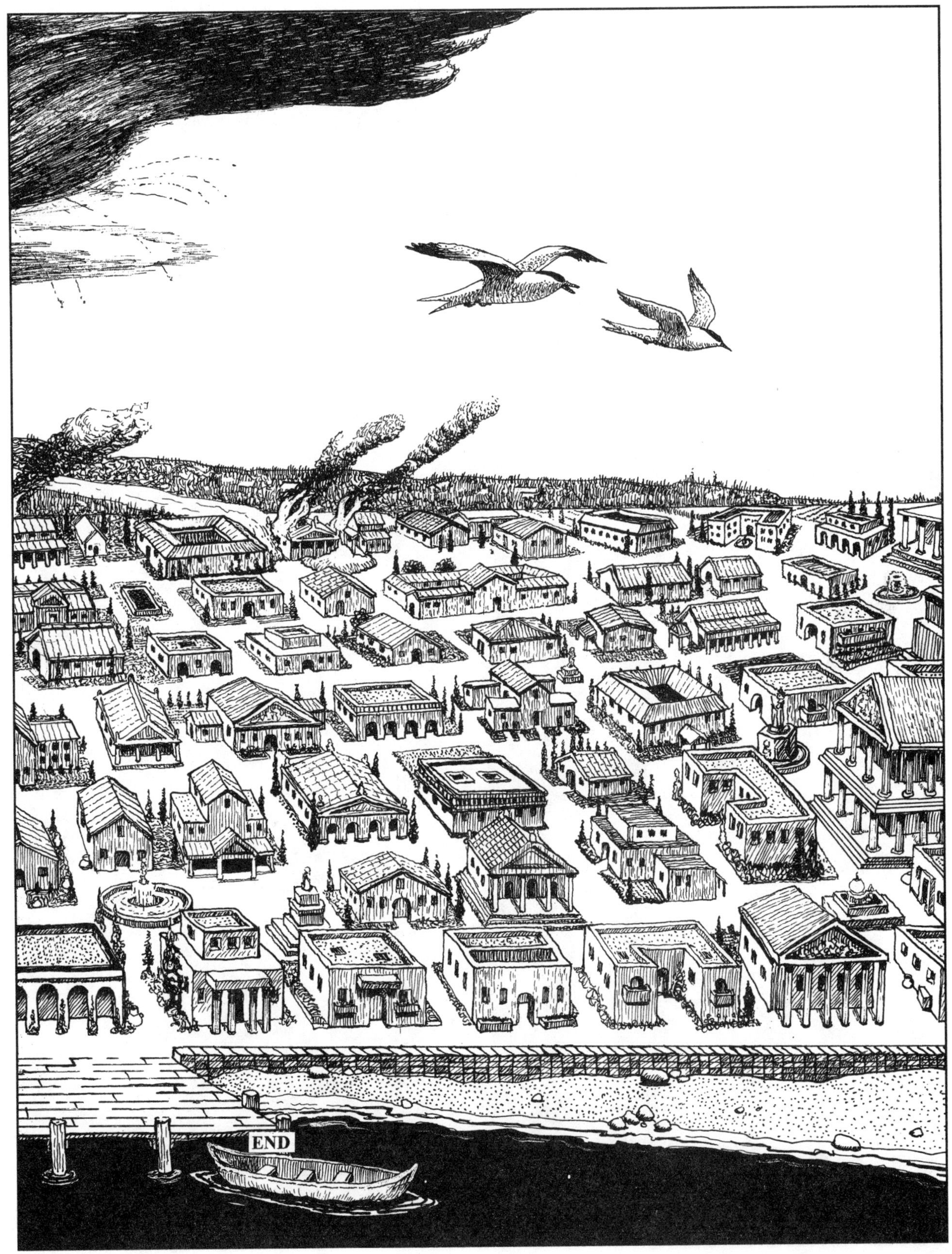
END

Mount Pelée

This eruption destroyed the port of St. Pierre on Martinique in 1902. Close obser-

vation shows that this is a spine volcano. Now that you've discovered this fact, descend in a hurry by finding a clear path to the bottom right corner.

Keep an Eye on Mount St. Helens

These sensors will monitor what's going on deep inside the volcano. Check each monitor for a reading by visiting each one only once-and do not backtrack.

Volcano I

Save the campers in their sleeping tents from the exploding Mount Saint Helens. Find a path to the tents, and then escape.

MT. SAINT HELENS
VIEWPOINT
PREVENT FOREST FIRES

CONGRATULATIONS

You have had a chance to see how devastating natural disasters can be. You have also demonstrated great courage by avoiding the tornados, hurricanes, earthquakes, volcanos, and other natural disasters to warn others of these dangers. As a result of your experiences, you will not flinch in the face of danger. That is good.

Fortunately, our planet is in a fairly pleasant mood most of the time. We can enjoy each day without fear that a disaster is on its way. But should the occasion arise for a warning to go out, you can expect a call.

Natural Disaster Guides

If you had any trouble finding your way through the mazes in this section, use the guides on the following pages. These guides should be used only in case of an emergency.

Releasing Weather Balloons

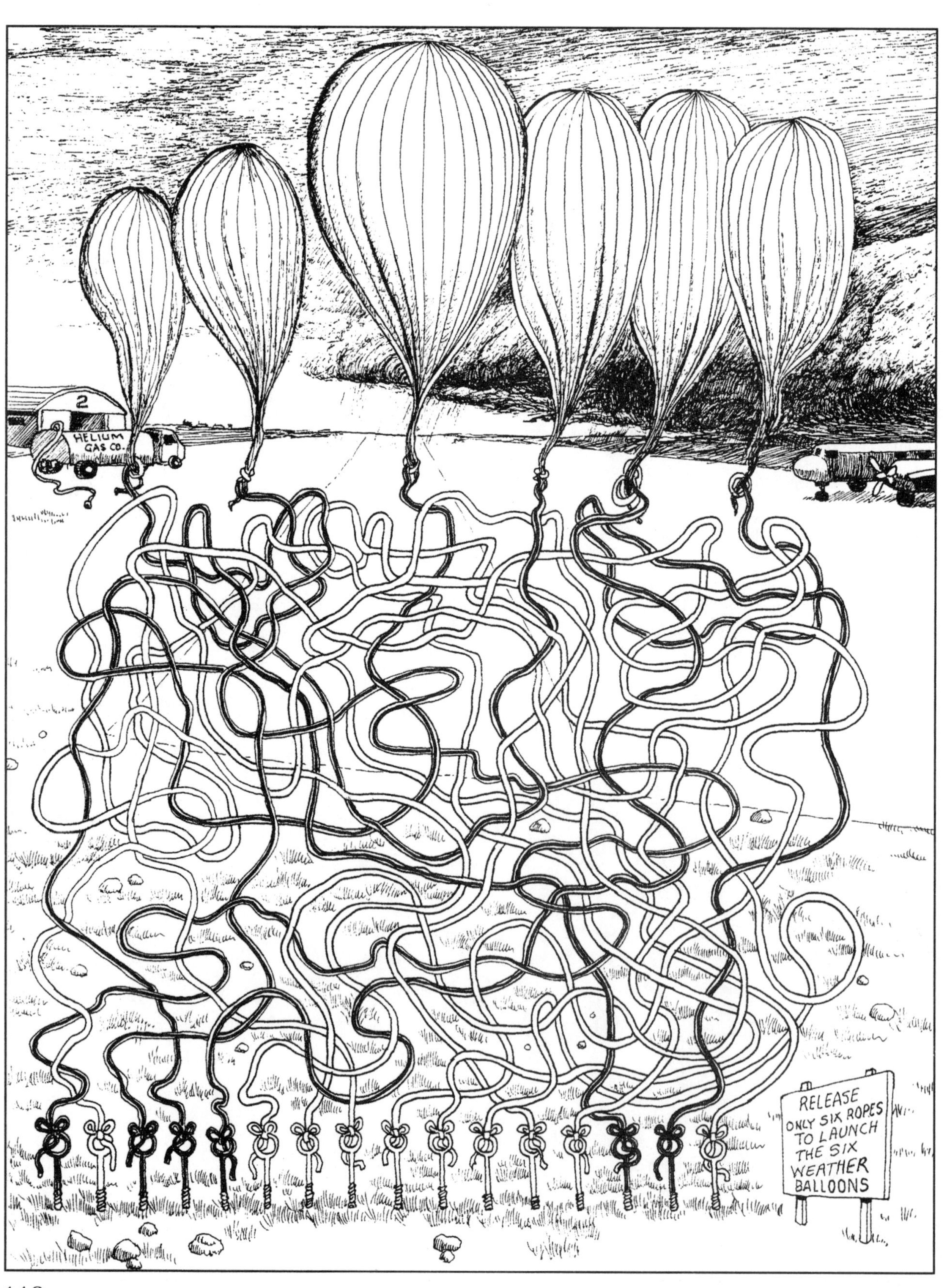

Tornado Warning I

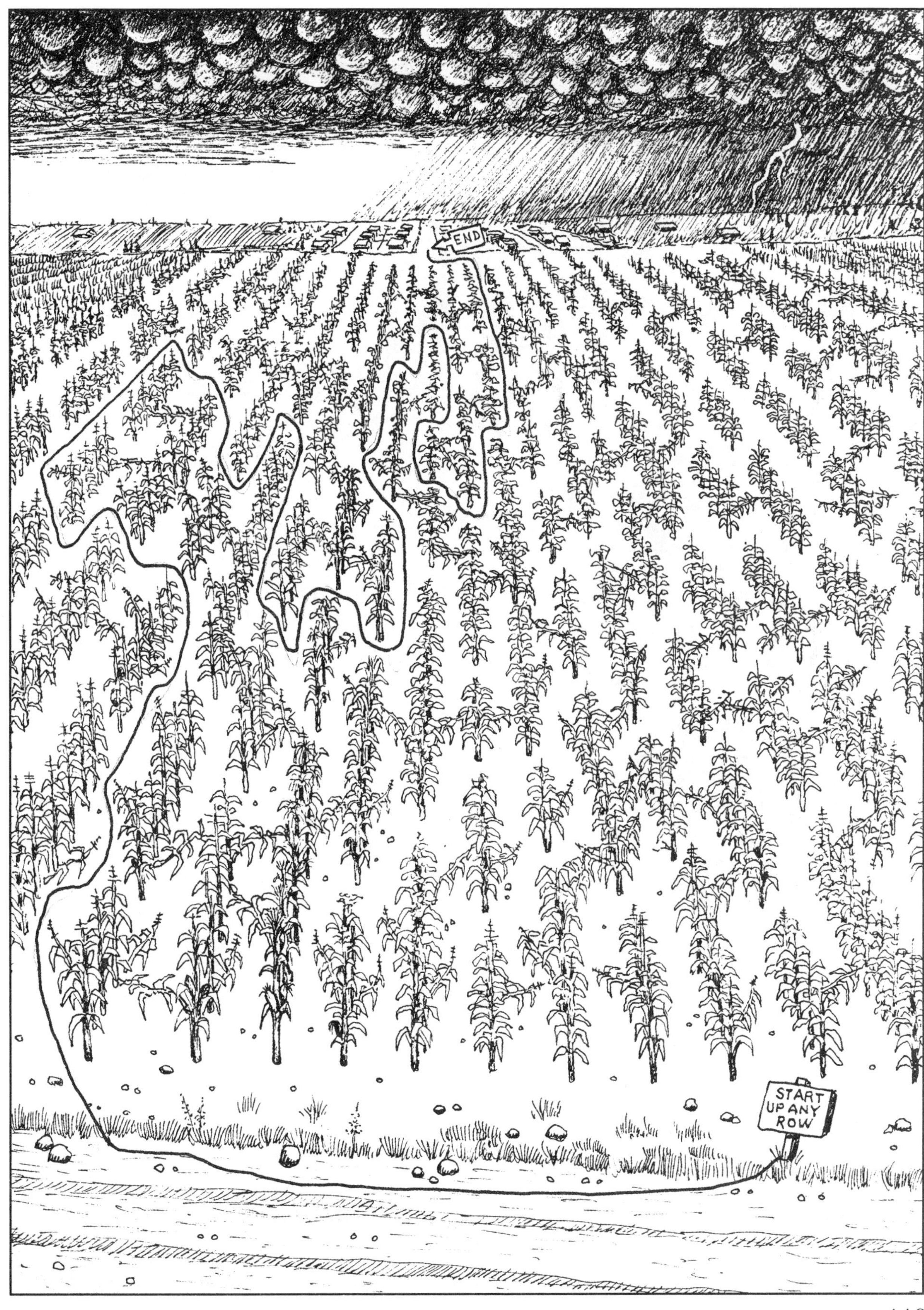

Tornado Warning II

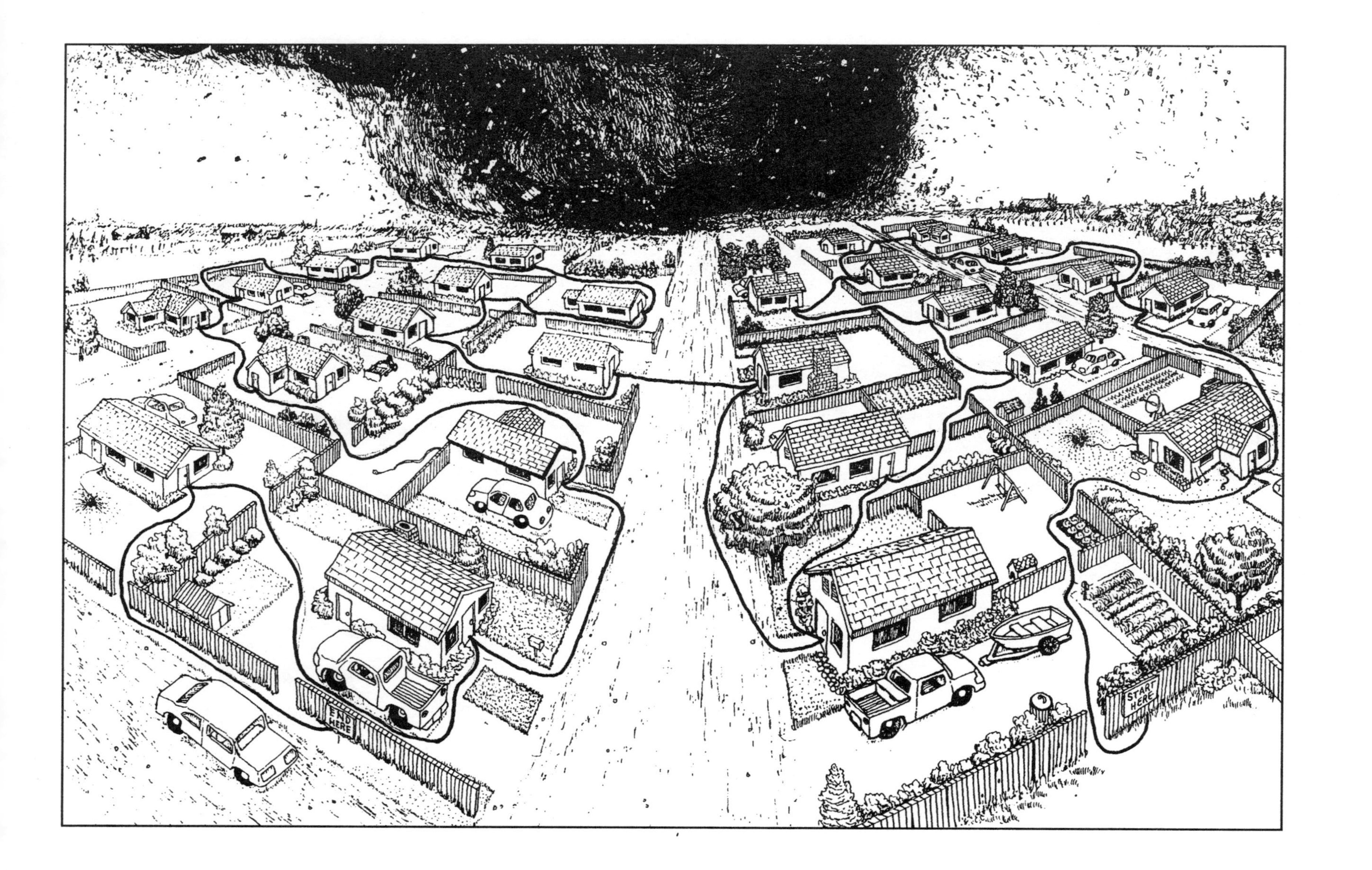

Escaping the Tornado

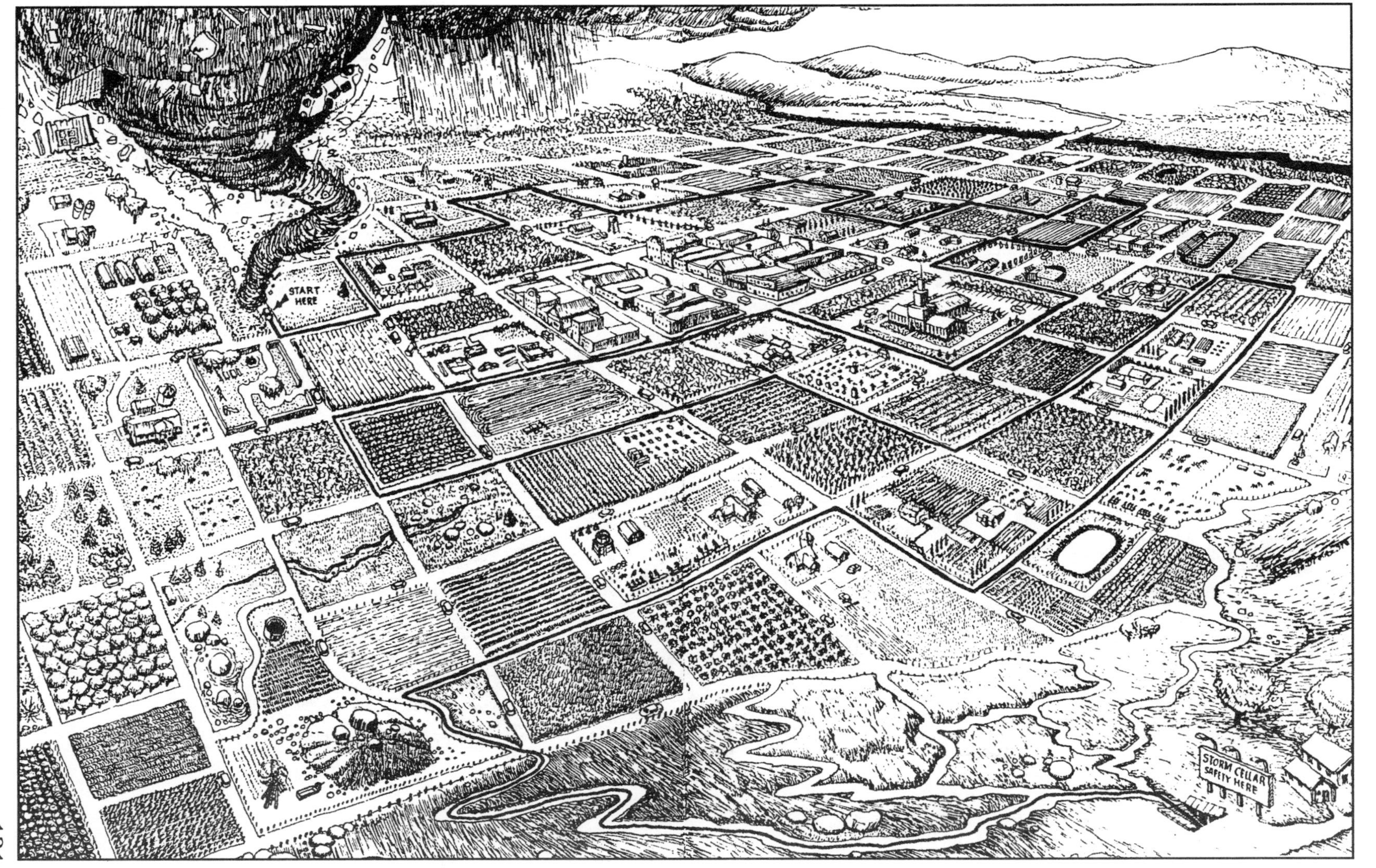

Finding the Hurricane's Center

Rescuing the Dog

Weather Satellite

Strengthening the Levee

Saving the Animals

Earthquake I

Shake, Rattle, and Roll

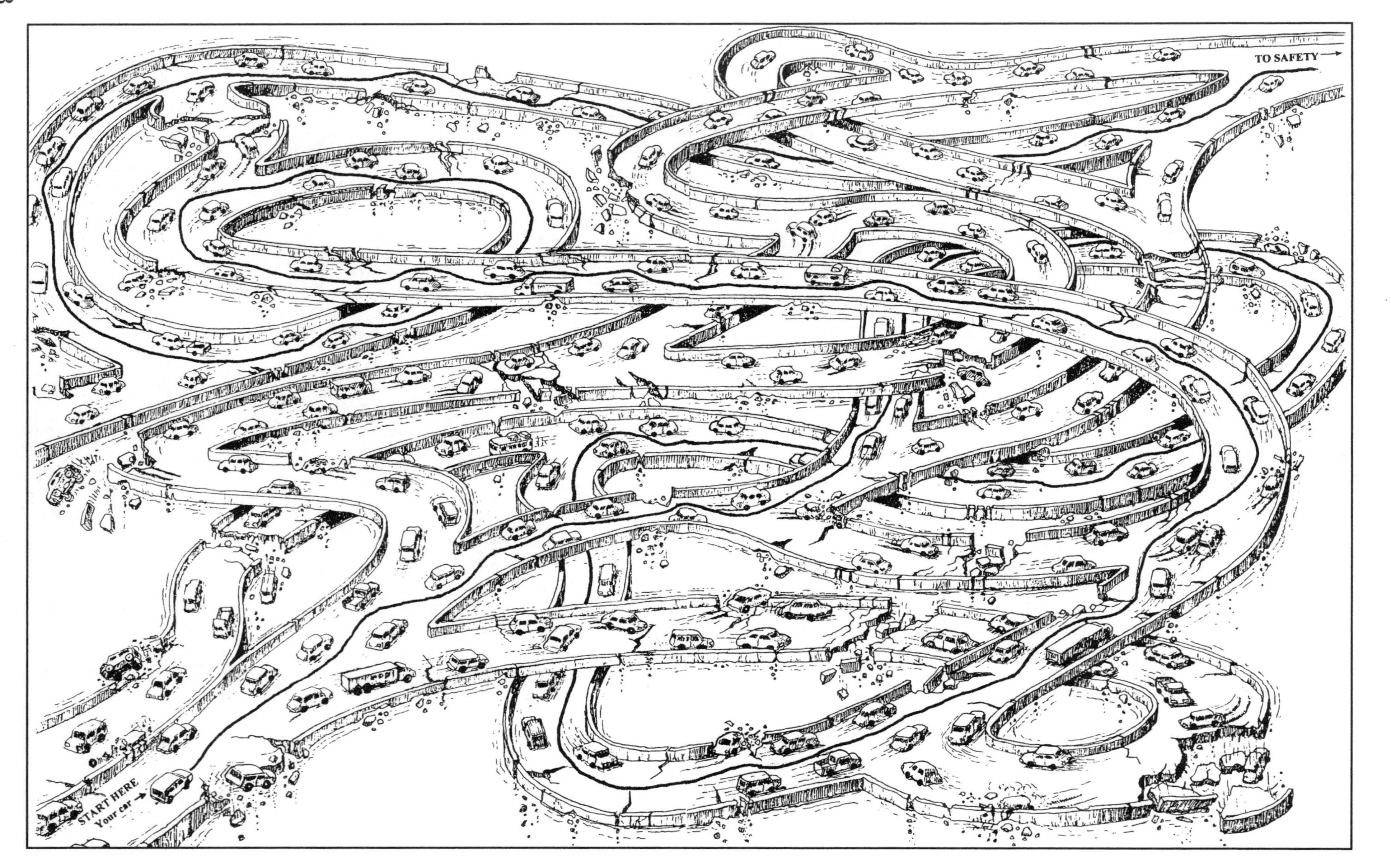

Shut Off the Gas

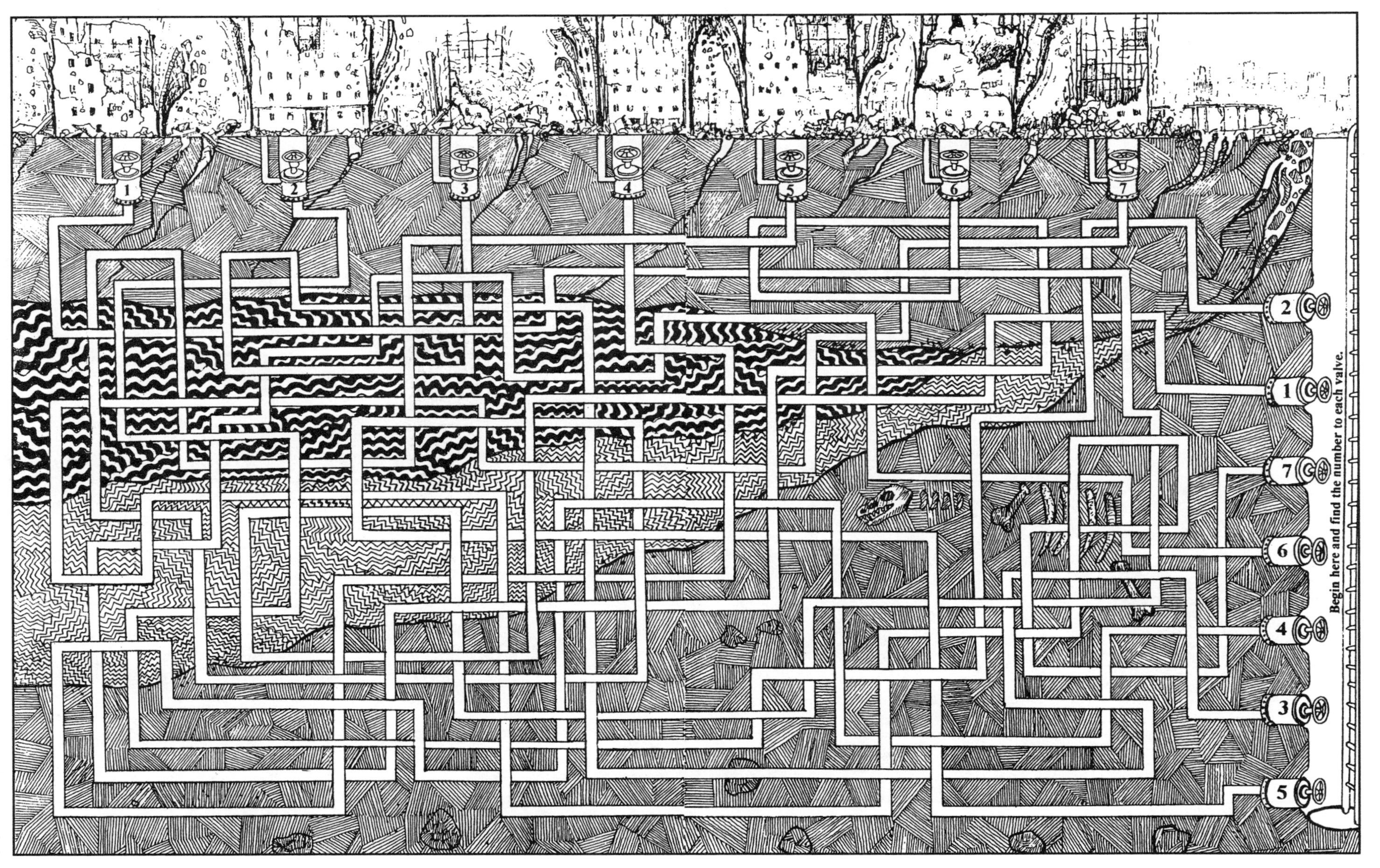

Demolished

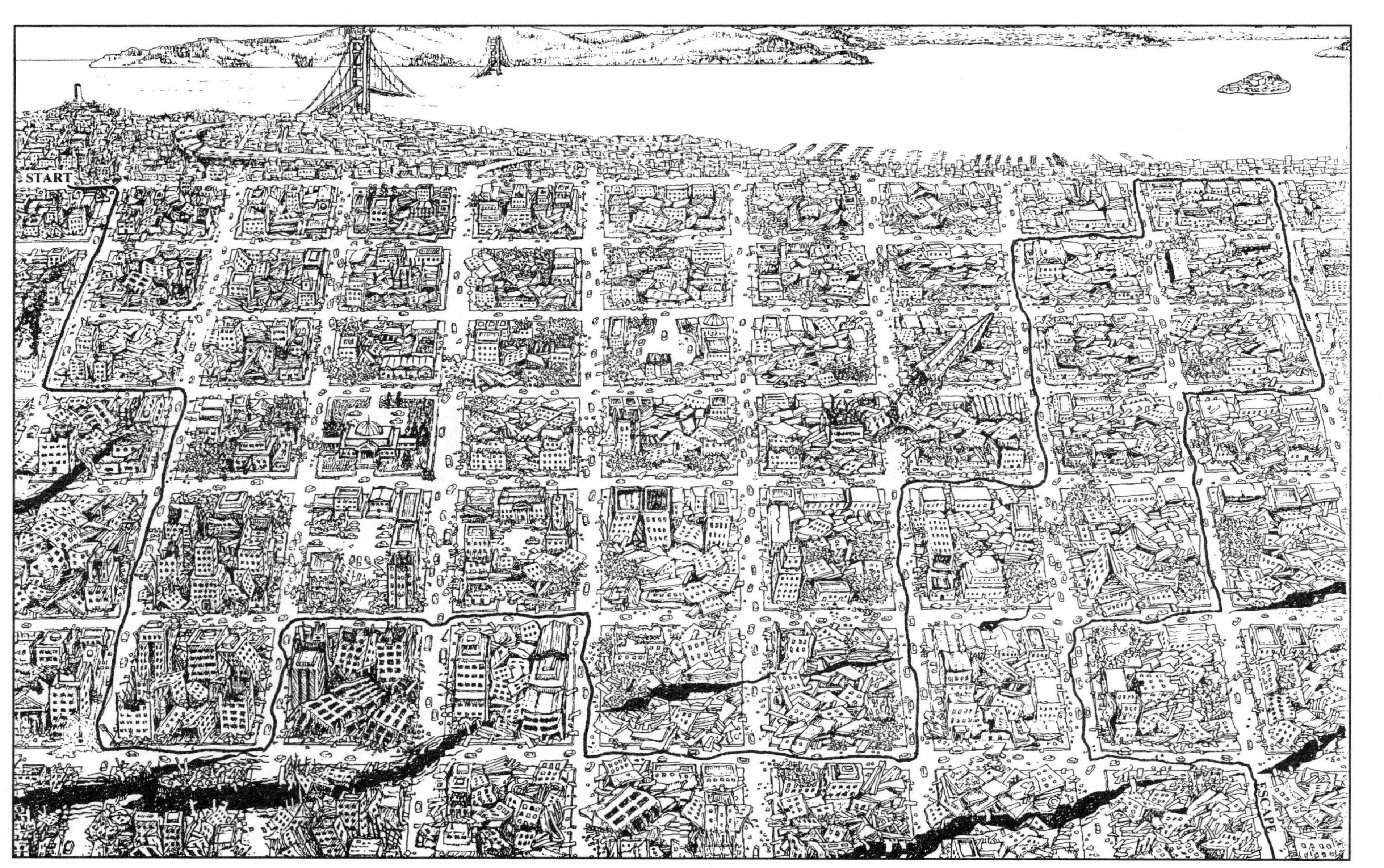

Earthquake Detection

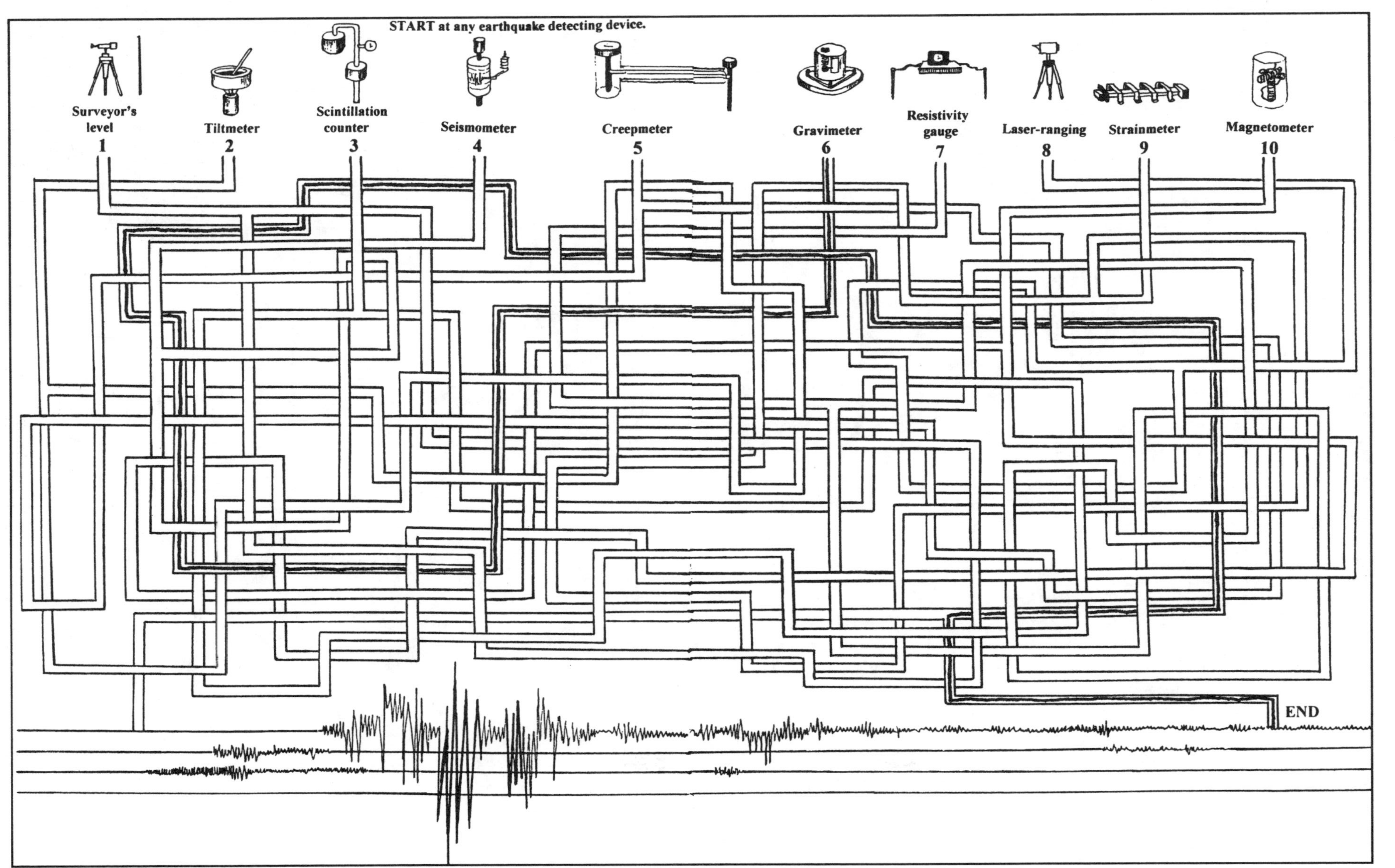

The Alaska Quake

Help!

Tsunami

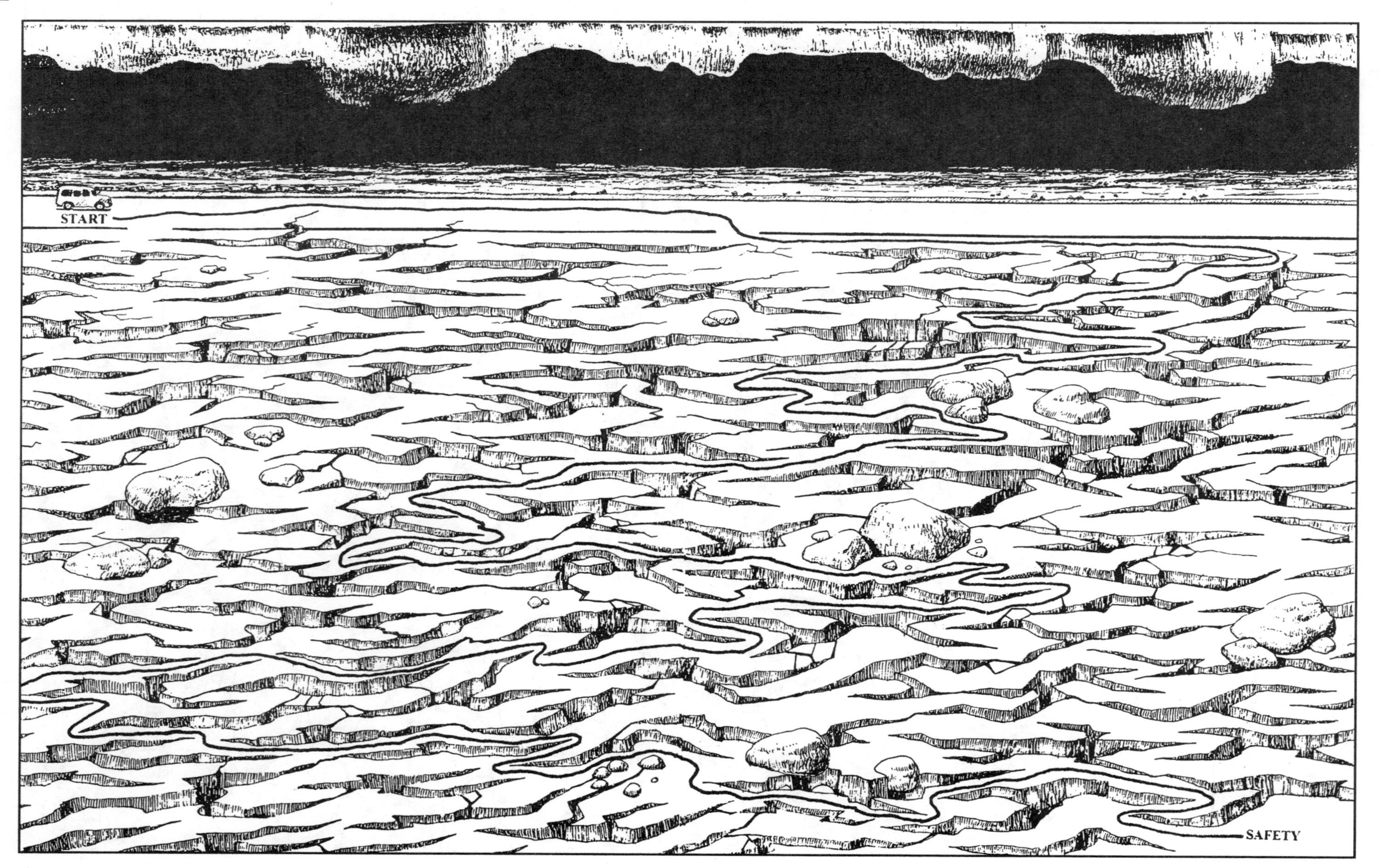

The Ruins

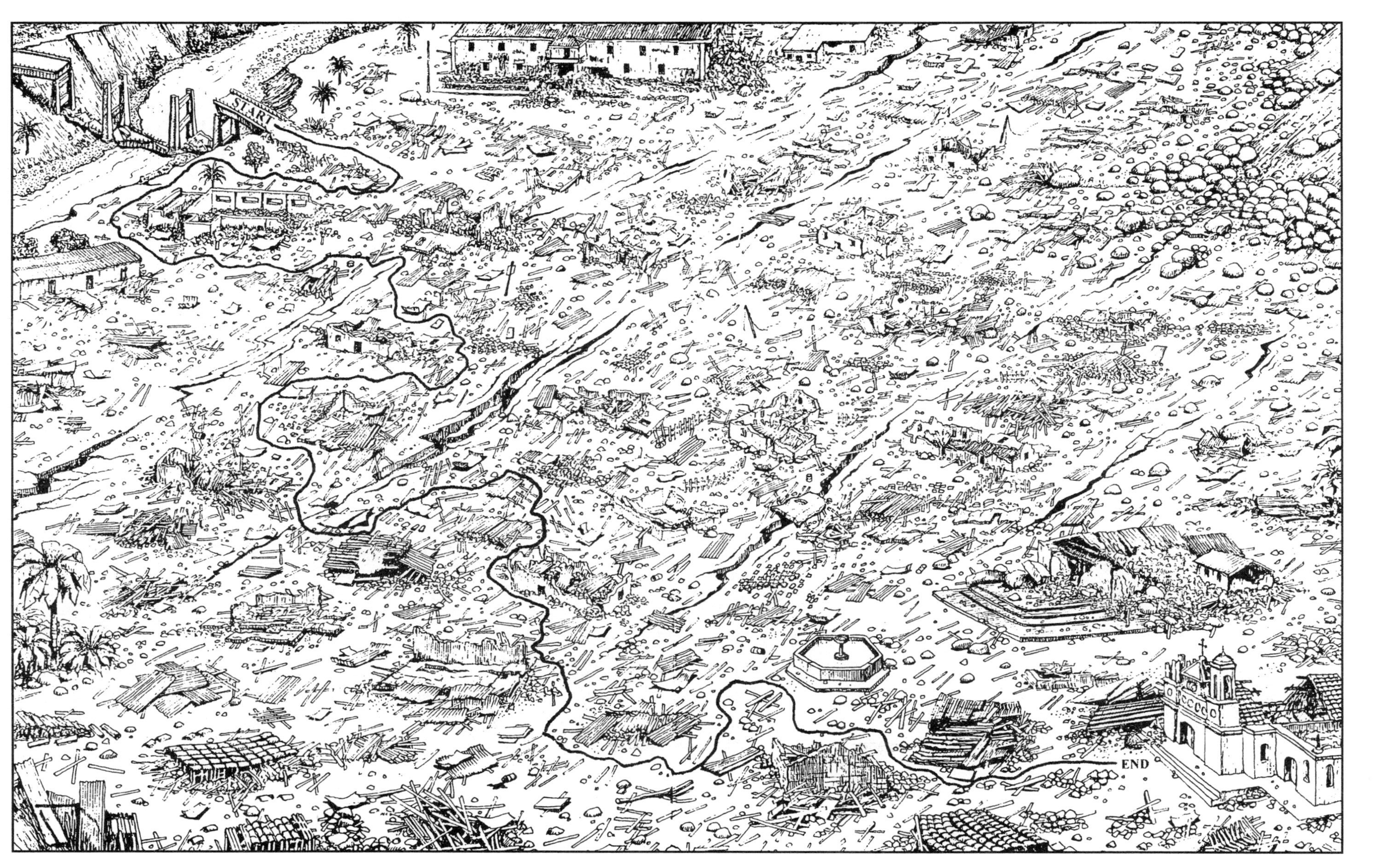

Tidal Wave

Preventing An Avalanche

Avalanche I

Avalanche II

Yellowstone National Park Fire

Planting Trees

Placing Probes

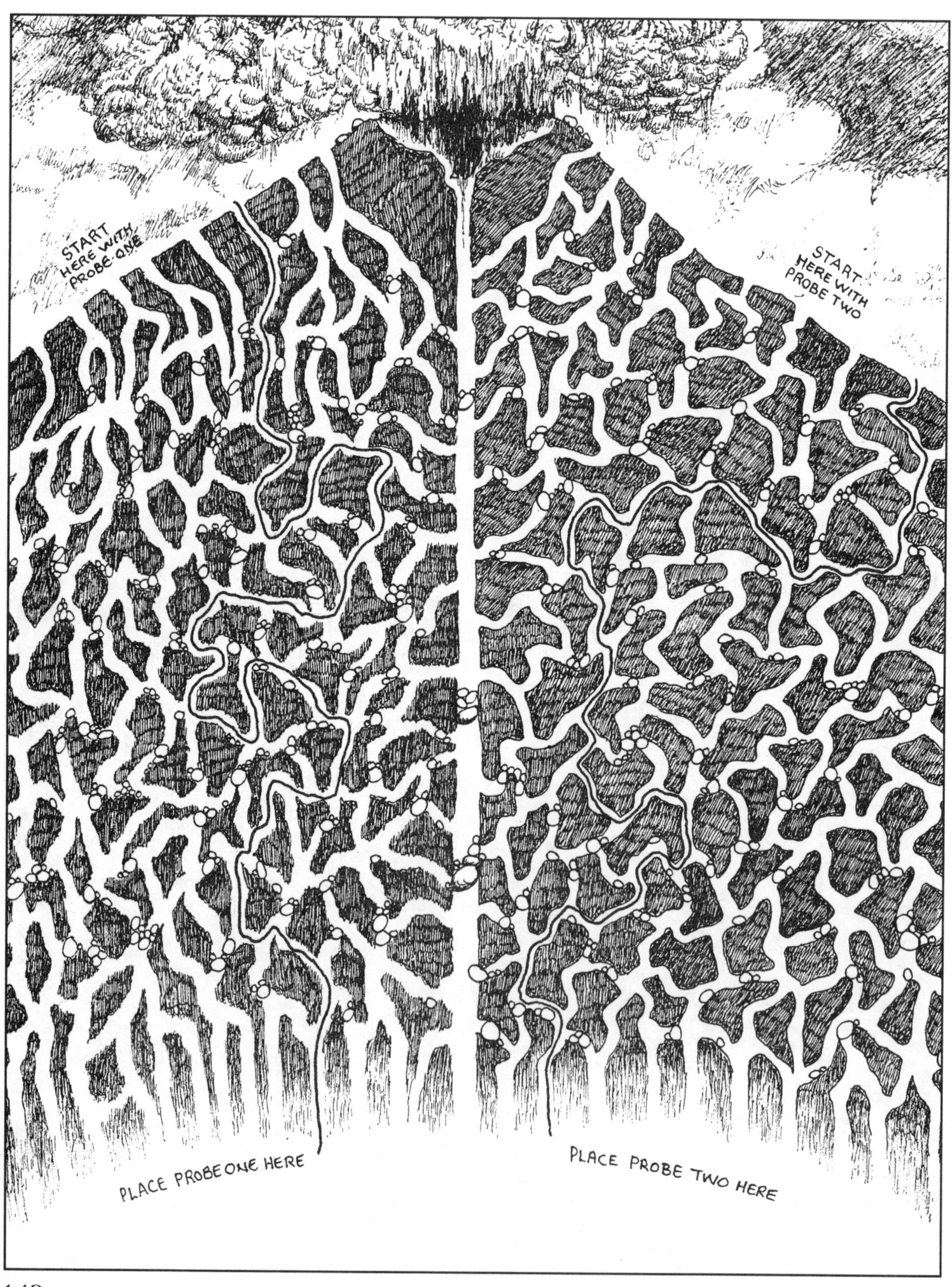

Placing a Sensor Probe

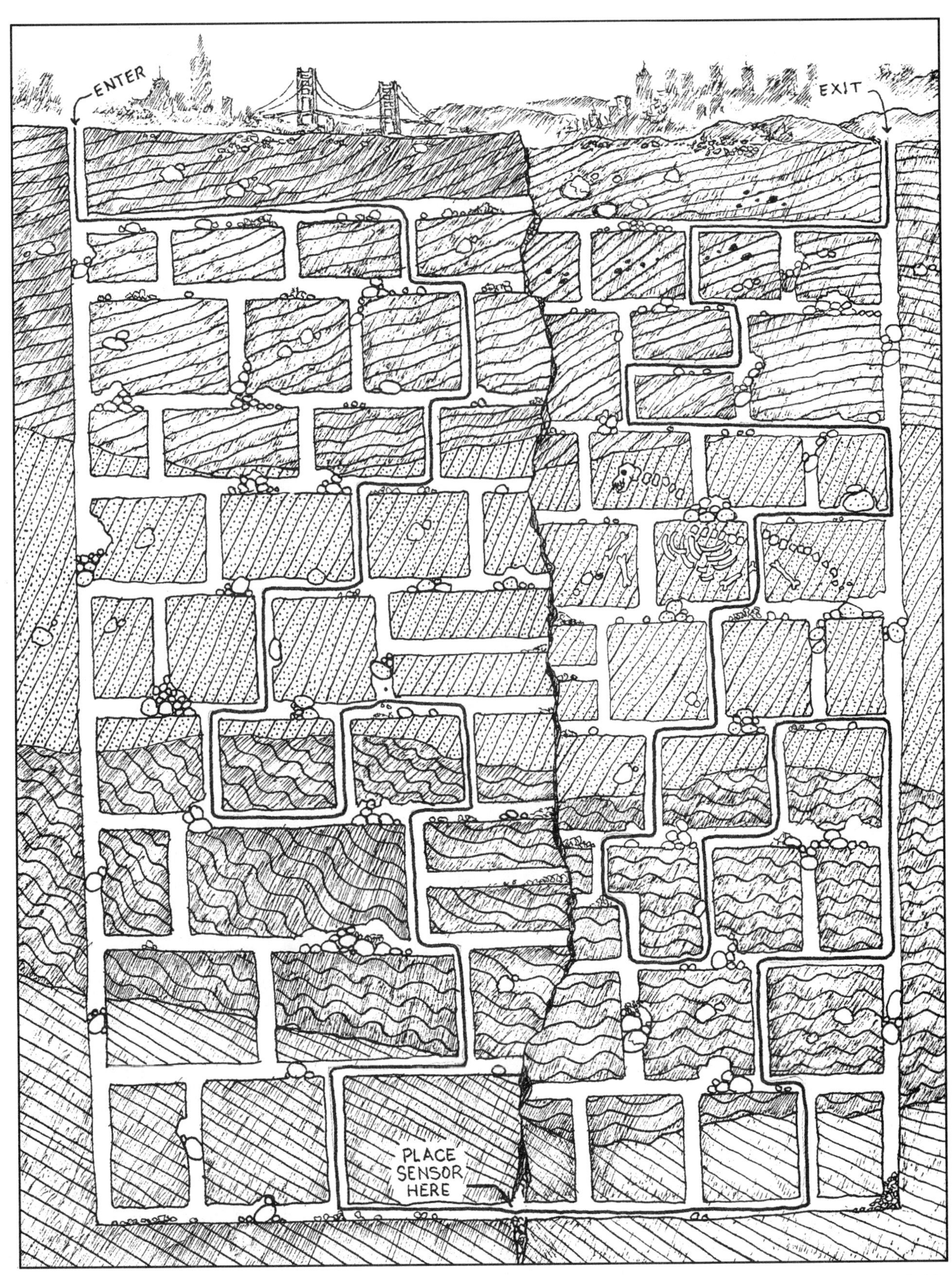

It Could Go Anytime!

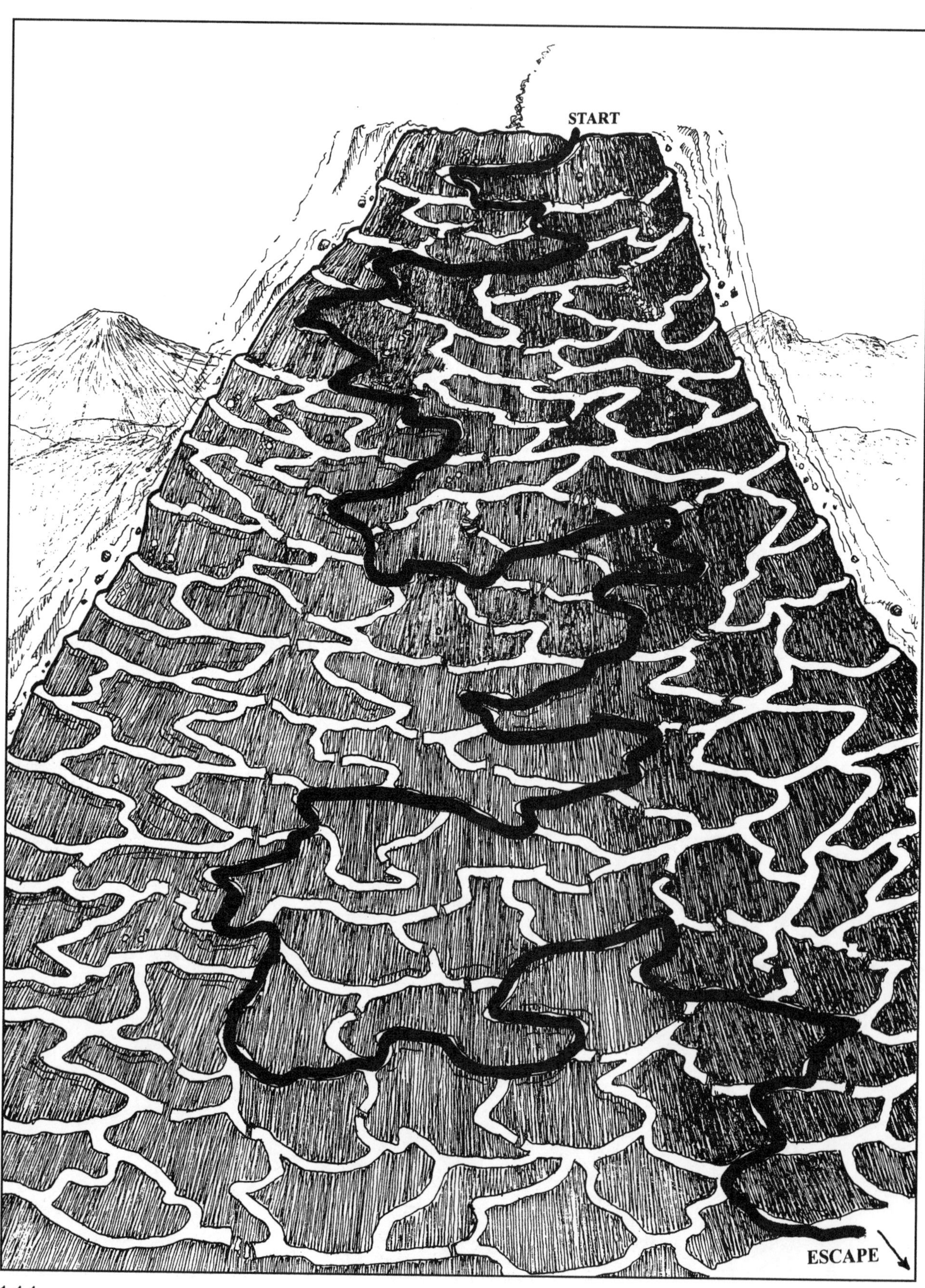

Volcano II

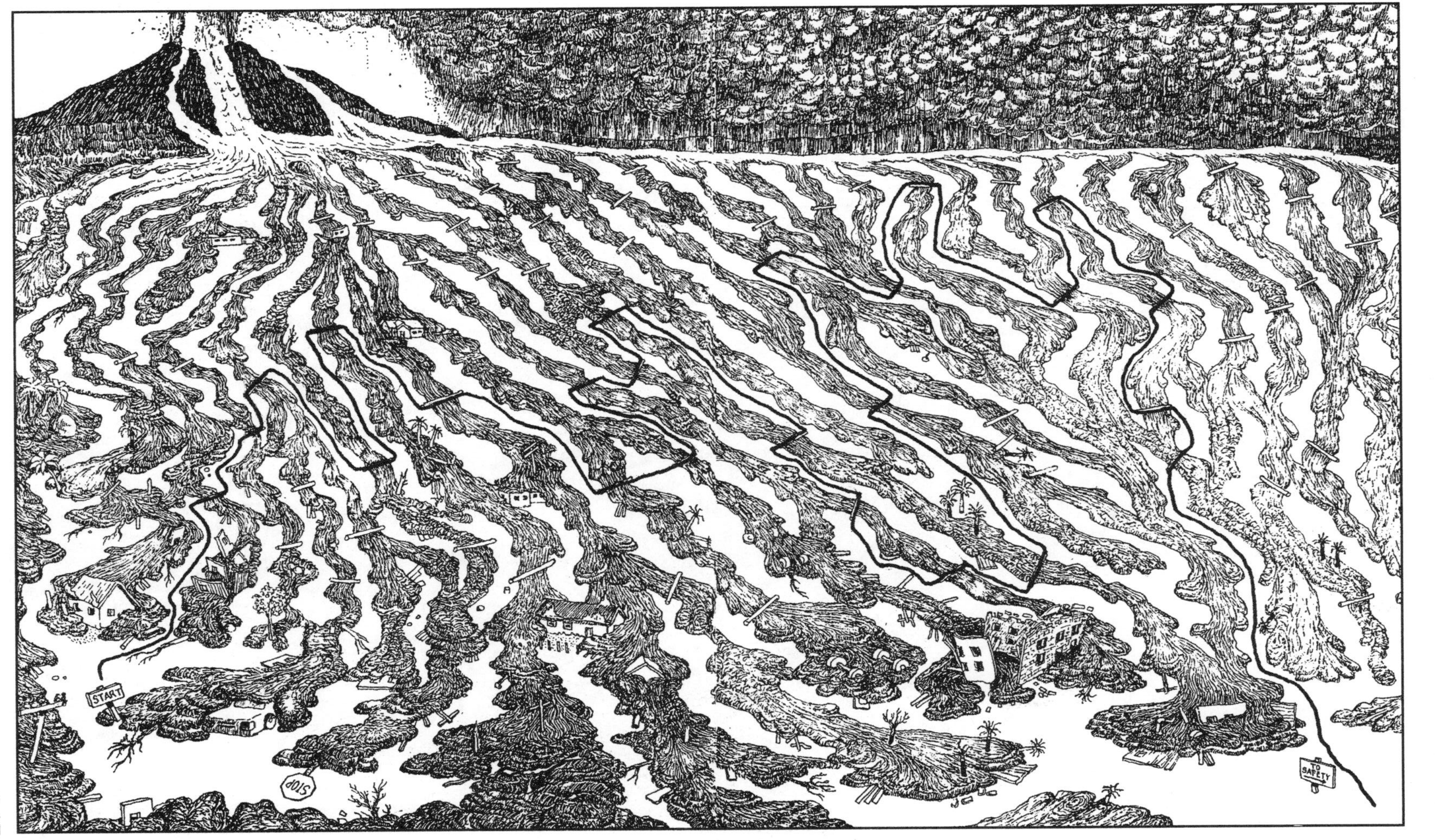

This Doesn't Look Good

The Calm Before the Eruption?

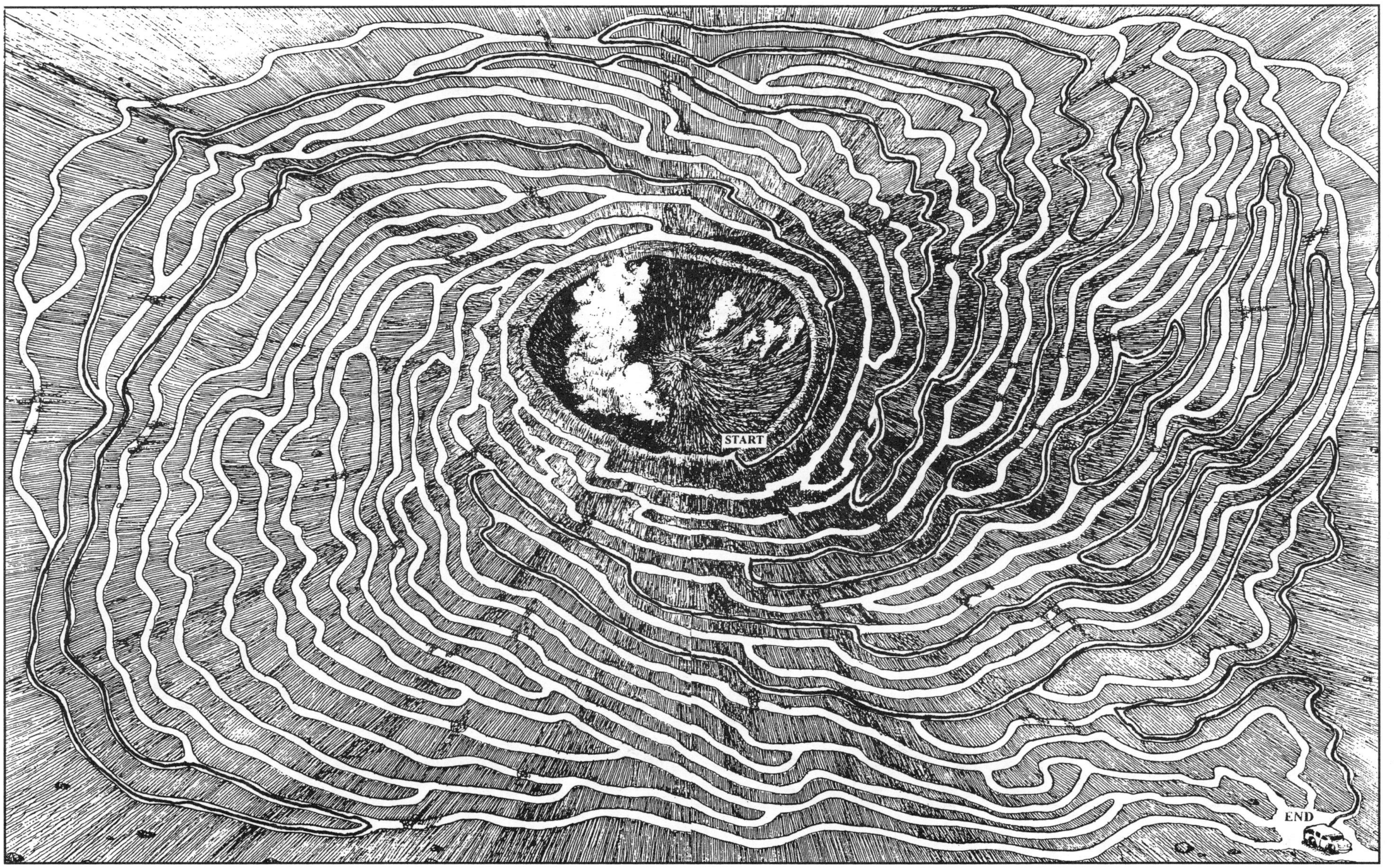

Mount Vesuvius

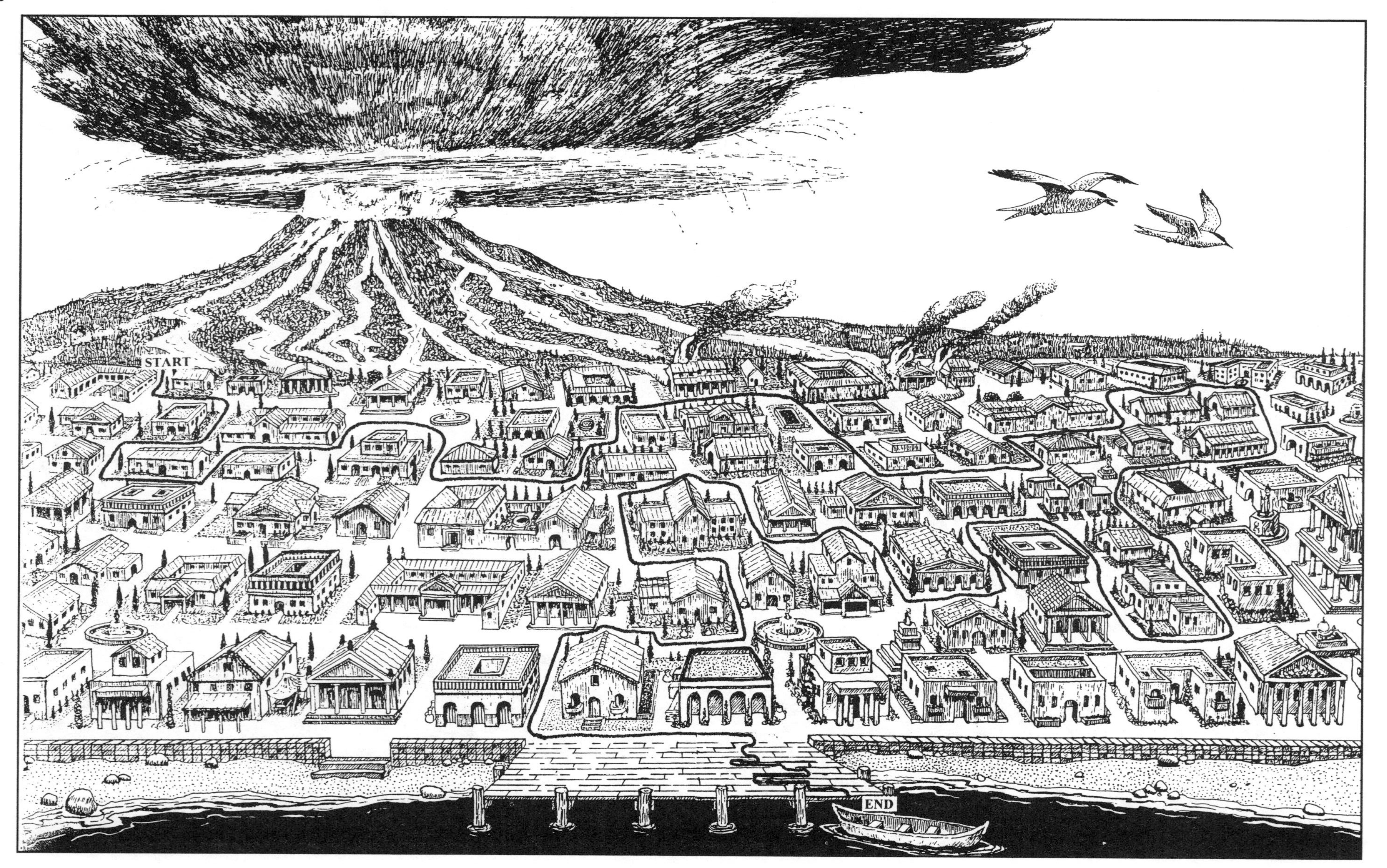

Mount Pelée

Keep an Eye on Mount St. Helens

Volcano I

MT. SAINT HELENS
VIEWPOINT
PREVENT FOREST FIRES
CAMP
WIGWAG
START HERE
THIS WAY
TO
SAFETY

DINOSAUR MAZES

CONTENTS

Introduction

The period of time the dinosaurs flourished upon the earth is called the Mesozoic Era. It lasted for nearly 150 million years, from about 250 to 65 million years ago. That era is broken down into three time periods: the Triassic, Jurassic, and the Cretaceous. The Triassic period was a time when there was just one great continent called Pangaea. During the Jurassic period, Pangaea had divided into two large continents called Laurasia and Gondwanaland. In the Cretaceous period, these two continents continued to divide until the continents looked almost like they do today.

Nothing can strike fear into one's mind than the thought of coming face to face with a hungry, meat-eating dinosaur. In 1841, when Sir Richard Owen gave the name "dinosaur" to the bones that were being discovered, he must have imagined that kind of fear, because the name means "terrible lizard." From those fossils, and ones that have since been found, paleontologists have been able to reconstruct what these animals looked like. Thanks to the creative abilities of the movie industry, that terror is accentuated when we see realistic-looking dinosaurs live again on the screen. Fortunately, there is never any real danger.

Even though a lot is known about how dinosaurs generally looked, there are many specific characteristics that are imagined. What if someone could actually return to the Mesozoic Era and get real photographs? Think how valuable to the scientific world they would be. Now, thanks to special computer chips, it is possible to transport a willing photographer back to the age of the dinosaurs. Just put this chip into the computer and off you go! All that is needed is a volunteer.

How about you? There will be unbelievable dangers. It will take great courage. You will have to take with you a laptop computer in order to return. And don't forget your camera. Oh, and thanks for volunteering. To get under way, just turn the page.

The Keyboard Setup

Put all 11 letters onto the proper letter pad by following each pathway from the letter to the pad. Then type in the period of time you want to travel to. Next, press ENTER . . . if you dare!

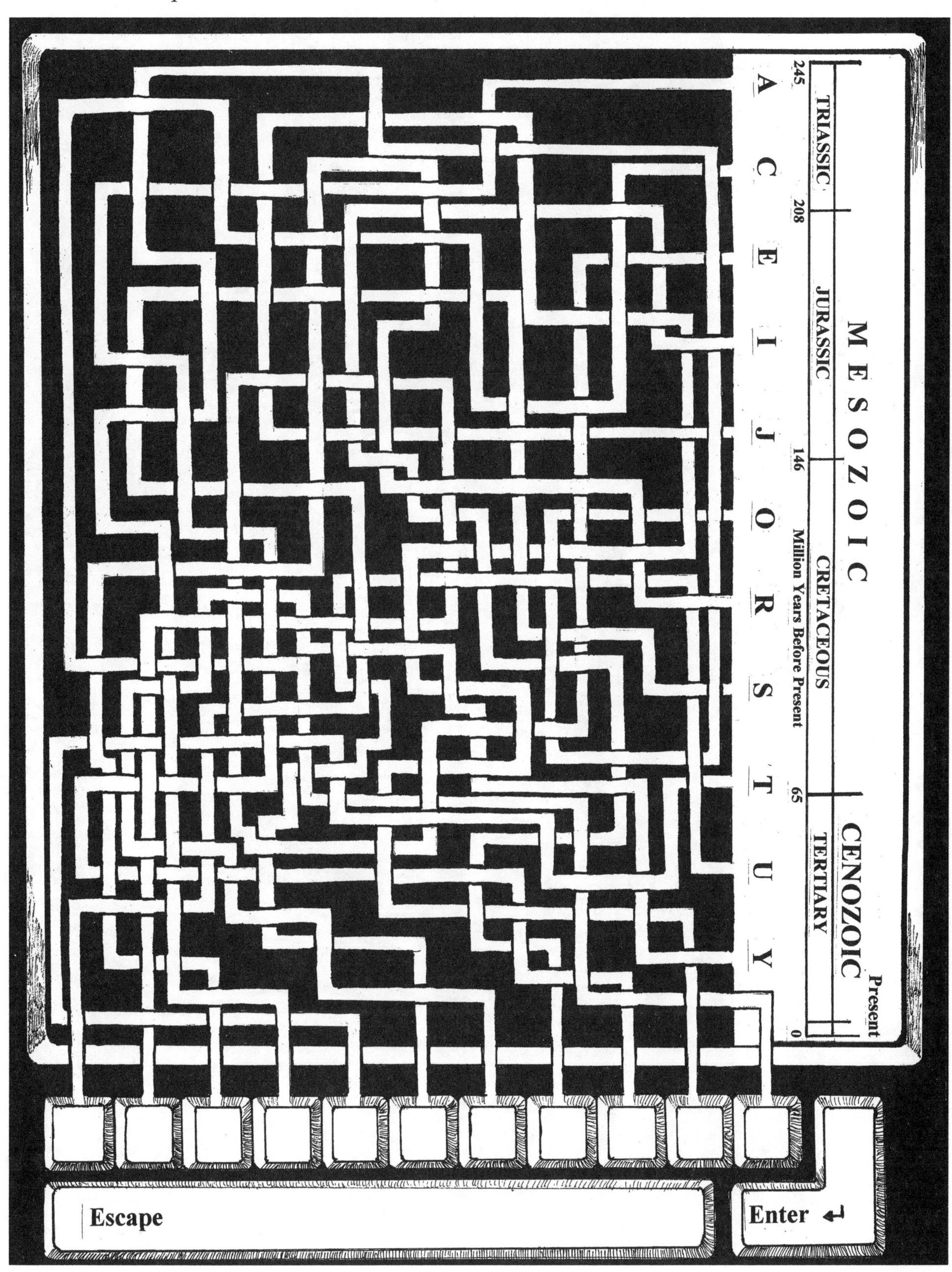

Allosaurus! Look Out!

It's obvious the transfer worked. This *Allosaurus* is looking for a meal. Set your lap-

top computer down to lighten your load. You can get it later. Keep your camera and escape from the dinosaur by avoiding the cracks.

Velociraptors!

This place doesn't look any safer than the last place you were at. Those raptors

have their eye on you. Find your way over the canyons to the rock cave for safety.

The Battle Is About to Begin

No time to waste here. This *Tyrannosaurus* and *Triceratops* have some real differences. Clear out fast by finding a clear path to the top of the hill.

Head to Head

Two *Pachycephalosaurus* are butting heads to win territory, while a third one awaits

his turn. You'd better move to the top of the hill while there's still time to find a clear path.

A Direct Hit

Euoplocephalus has made a direct hit that is bringing down this *Tyrannosaurus*. You've got 30 seconds to avoid the cracks and get out of the way.

ESCAPE →

An Aerial Threat

These *Rhamphorhynchus* are looking for food that crosses into a shadow. Rapidly cross this area by staying in the sunlight.

END

The Nest

This is a tender scene. This mother *Maiasaura* is asleep. Get a photo of each egg by

finding a path to each egg without backtracking or crossing over your own trail. Hurry bcforc that dragonfly lands on mother's nose and she awakes.

Feed the Brontosaurus

This plant eater is friendly if you feed him. Find the vine that will get you to the limb, feed him some leaves, and take a close-up photo before you descend.

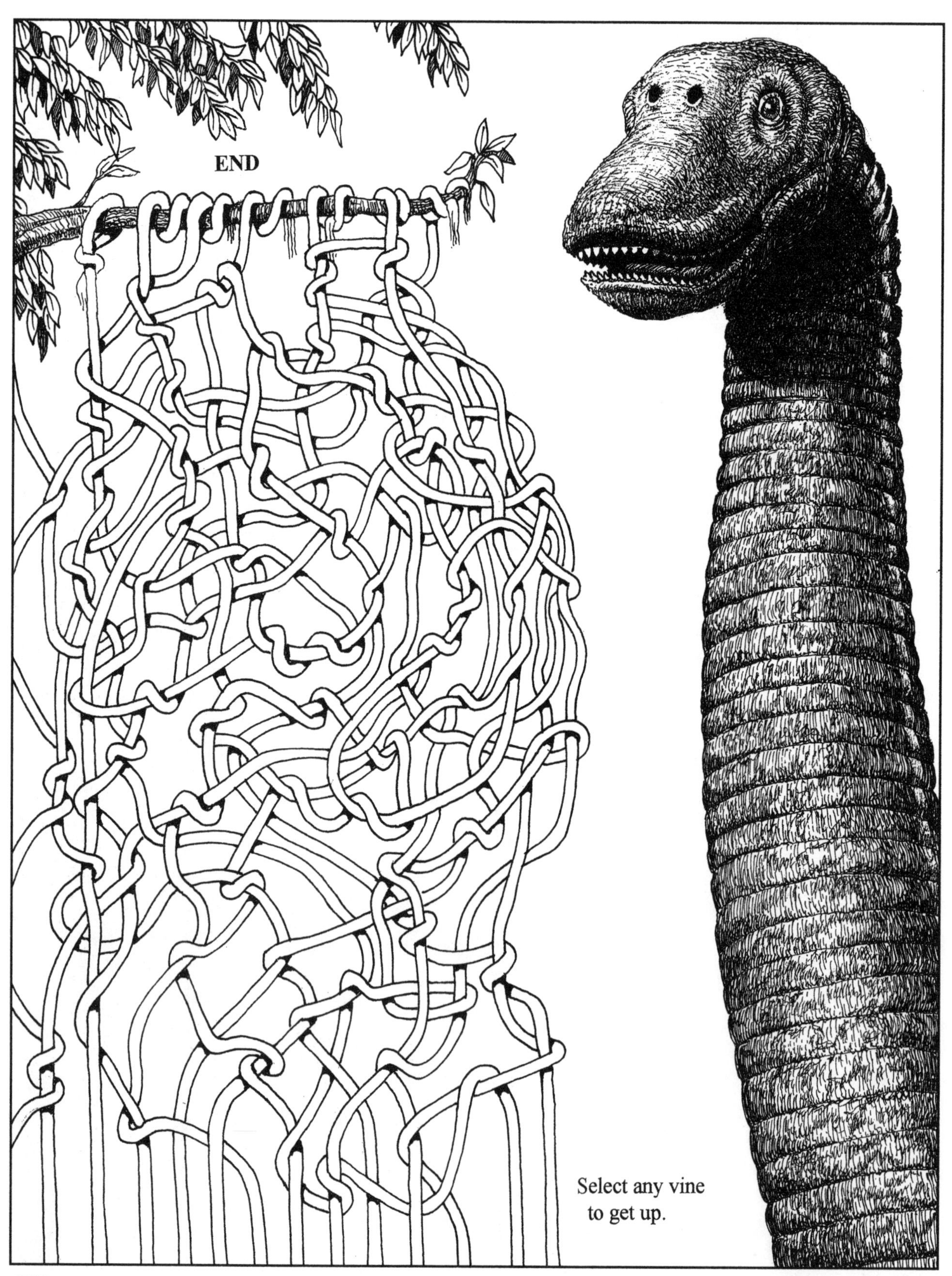

The Welcoming Committee

You'd better choose wisely when you select the vine for your descent. Each one of the raptors is hoping for a meal.

The Tar Pit

A *Stegosaurus* is sinking into this tar pit while its mate looks on. Move out onto the connecting logs to get a close-up photo and then exit on the right.

END

Photograph the Nest

While the adult *Pteranodon* is looking for food, climb the connecting rocks and photograph the babies. Be careful not to drop your camera.

Retrieve Your Camera

Your falling camera has knocked out a nesting *Pteranodon.* Descend the connecting rocks to pick up your camera before he awakes.

Create a Fossil Bed

This is a potential fossil bed if you can remove that fallen tree to let the mud flow

over these remains. As you make your way to the tree, don't touch any of the remains.

Earthquake

During these prehistoric times, earthquakes were common. Find your way to solid ground near the shaking tree. Avoid the cracks.

SAFETY HERE

Volcanic Eruption

It's raining hot rocks from that distant volcano. You have 30 seconds to find a clear path around the dinosaurs and get out of this place.

ESCAPE

The End Is Near

A huge asteroid that will end the dinosaur era—and you—is near impact. Your

laptop computer is where you left it when you arrived. Avoid the dinosaurs, get to it as fast as you can, and hit ENTER. Good luck!

CONGRATULATIONS

What you have accomplished will go down in history as equal to, if not greater than, any of the great explorations—including exploring the mysteries of the great oceans and walking on the moon. Your photographs will be in every publication. You will be honored by leading scientists, top universities, and world leaders.

More important, you have demonstrated great courage and a willingness not to give up even in the face of the most terrifying of circumstances. You are to be greatly admired. Now, see if you can find someone else who is willing to volunteer as you did and go back to the Mesozoic Era. The world can always use more photographs. Just crank up the computer and away they'll go.

Special Guides for the Mesozoic Era

If you had any trouble finding your way, you can refer to the guides on the following pages. It is doubtful, however, if you had trouble, that you survived.

The Keyboard Setup

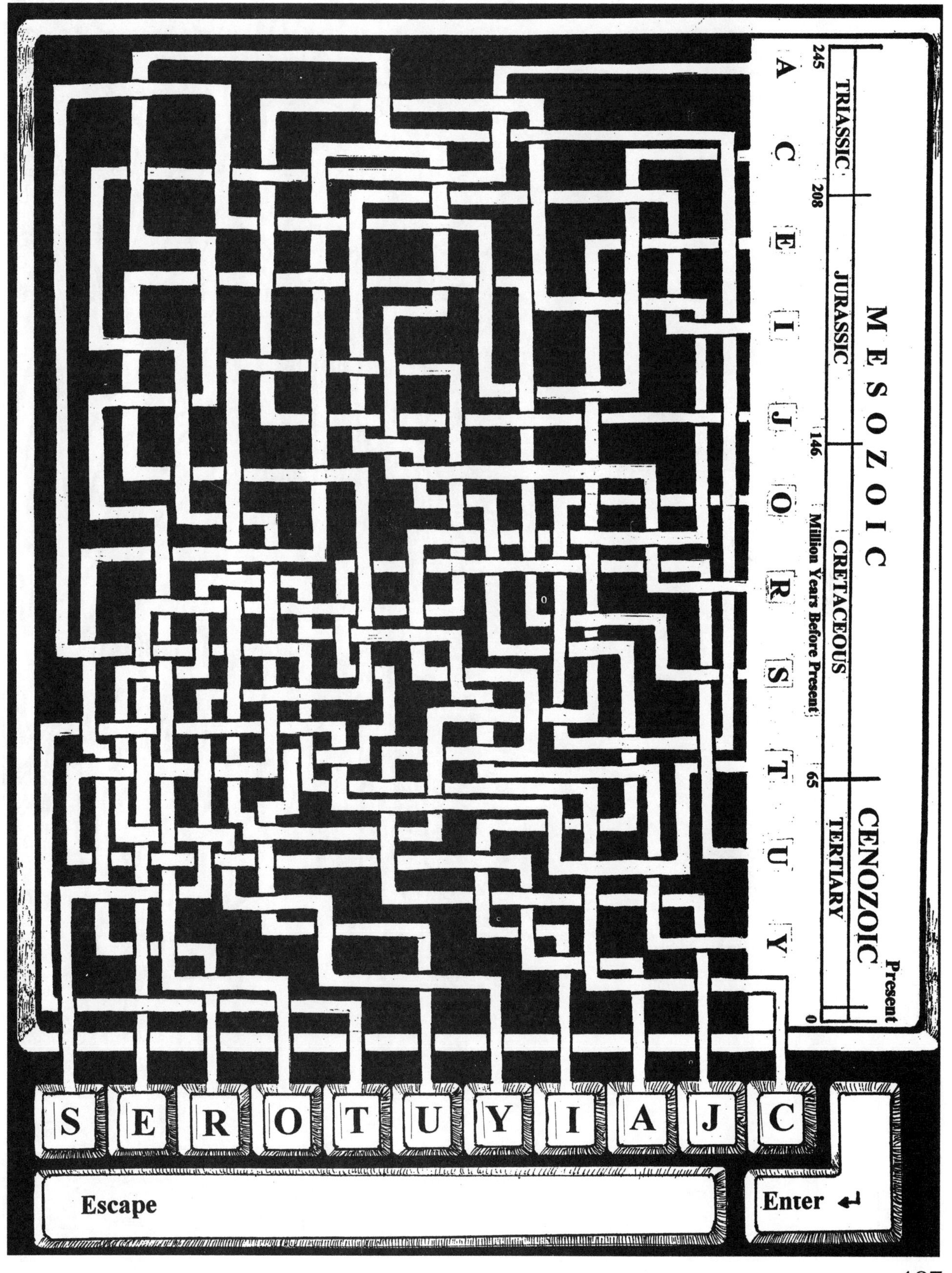

Allosaurus! Look Out!

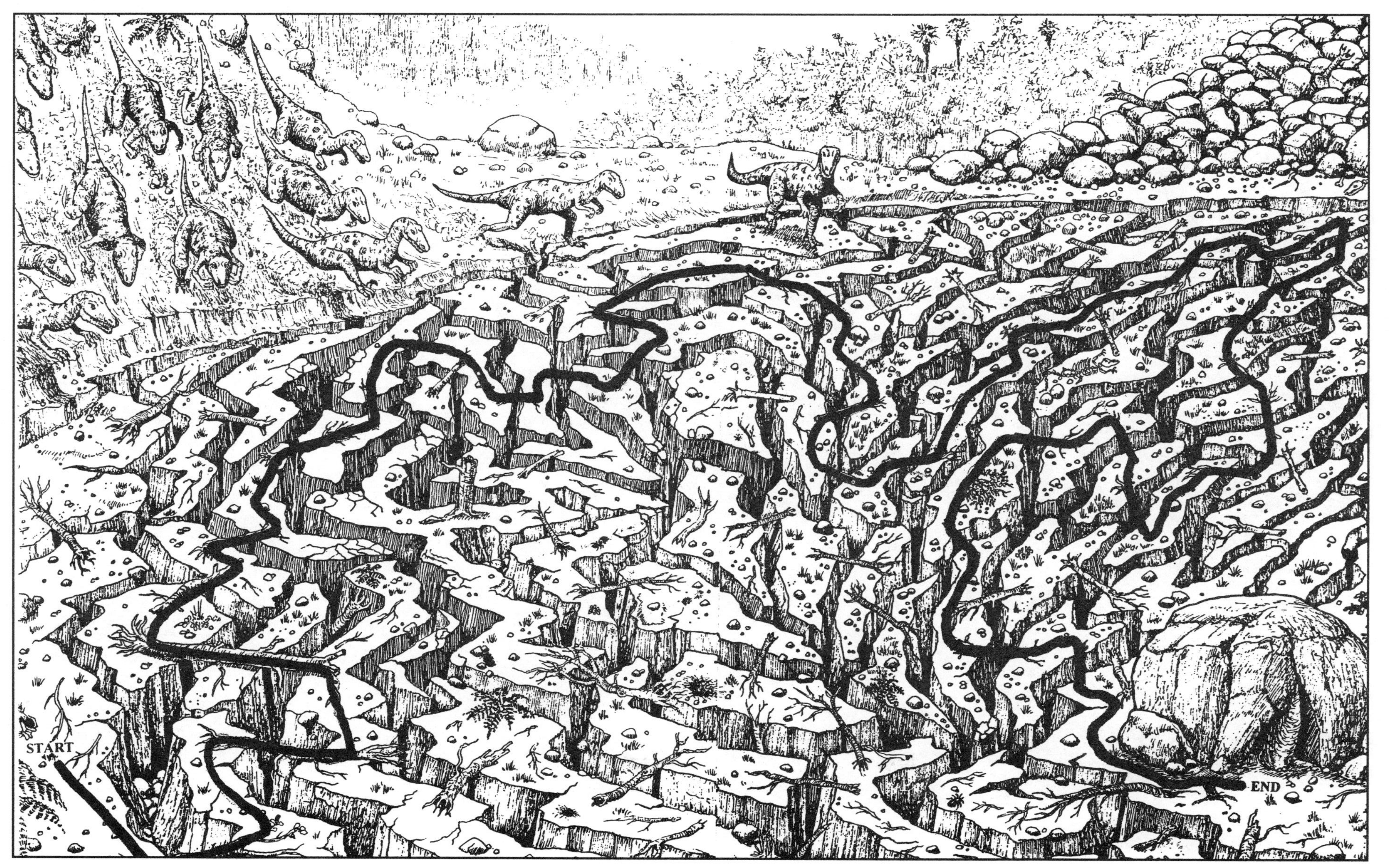
START
END

The Battle Is About to Begin

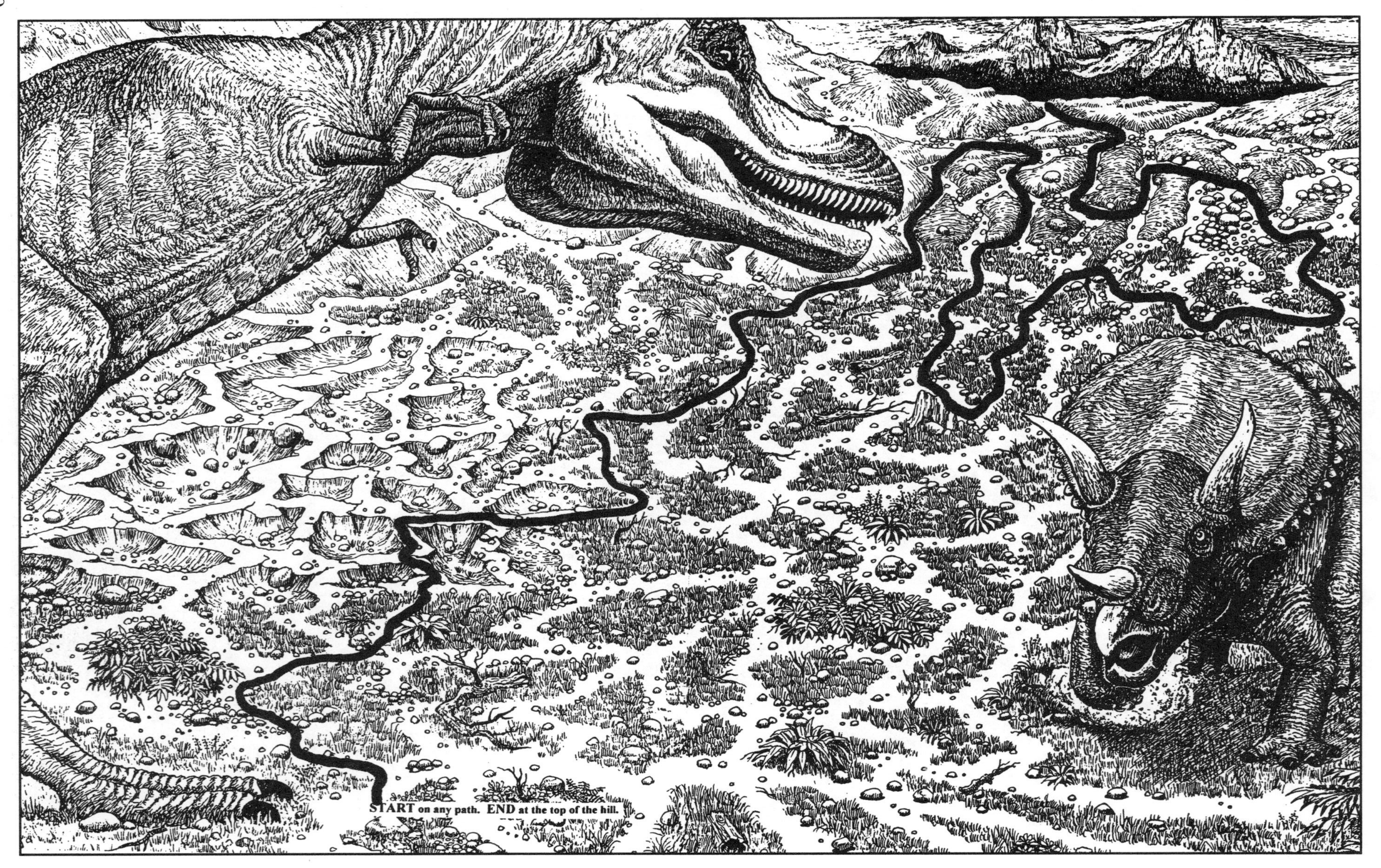

Head to Head

START
ESCAPE

An Aerial Threat

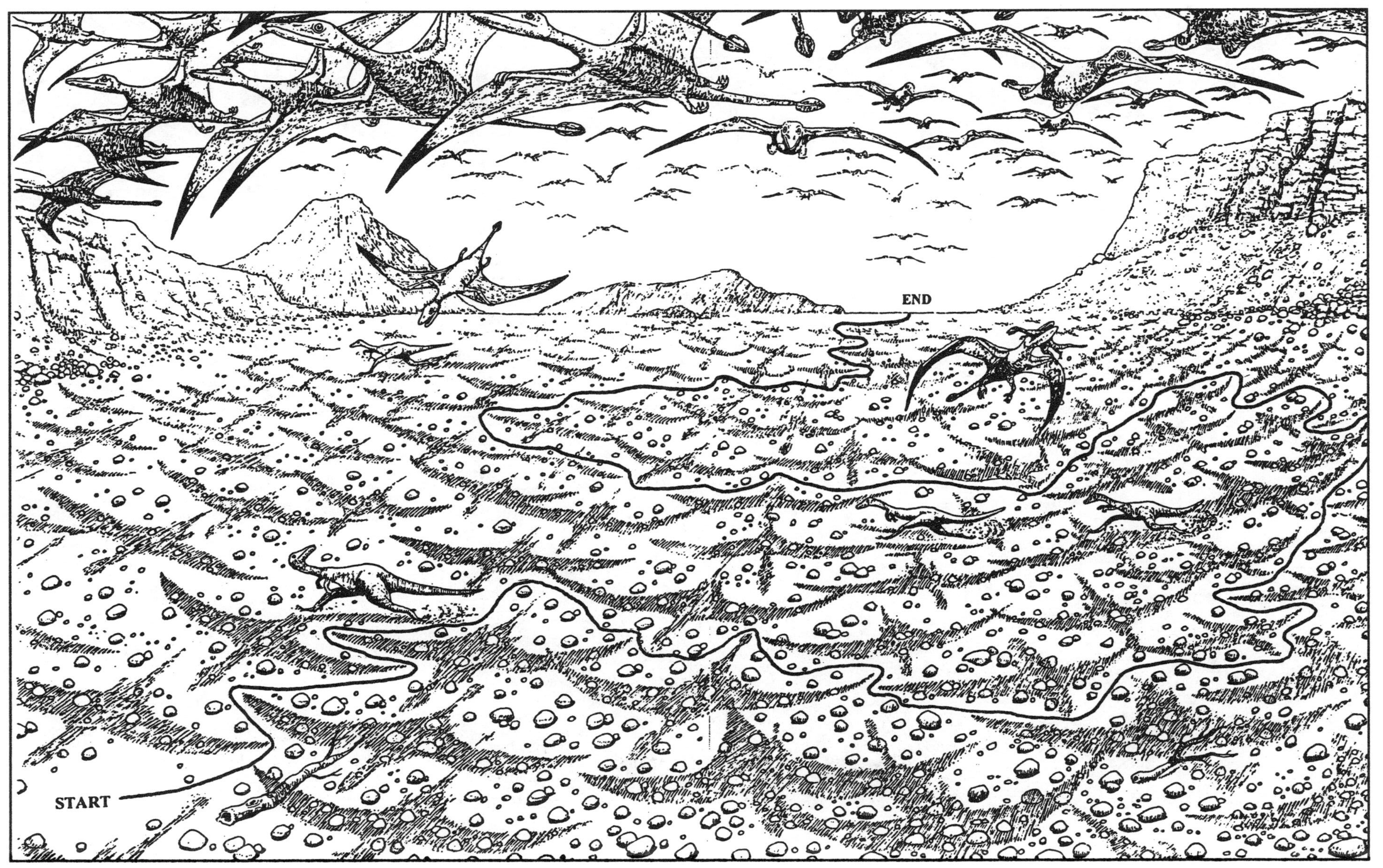

START
END

Feed the Brontosaurus

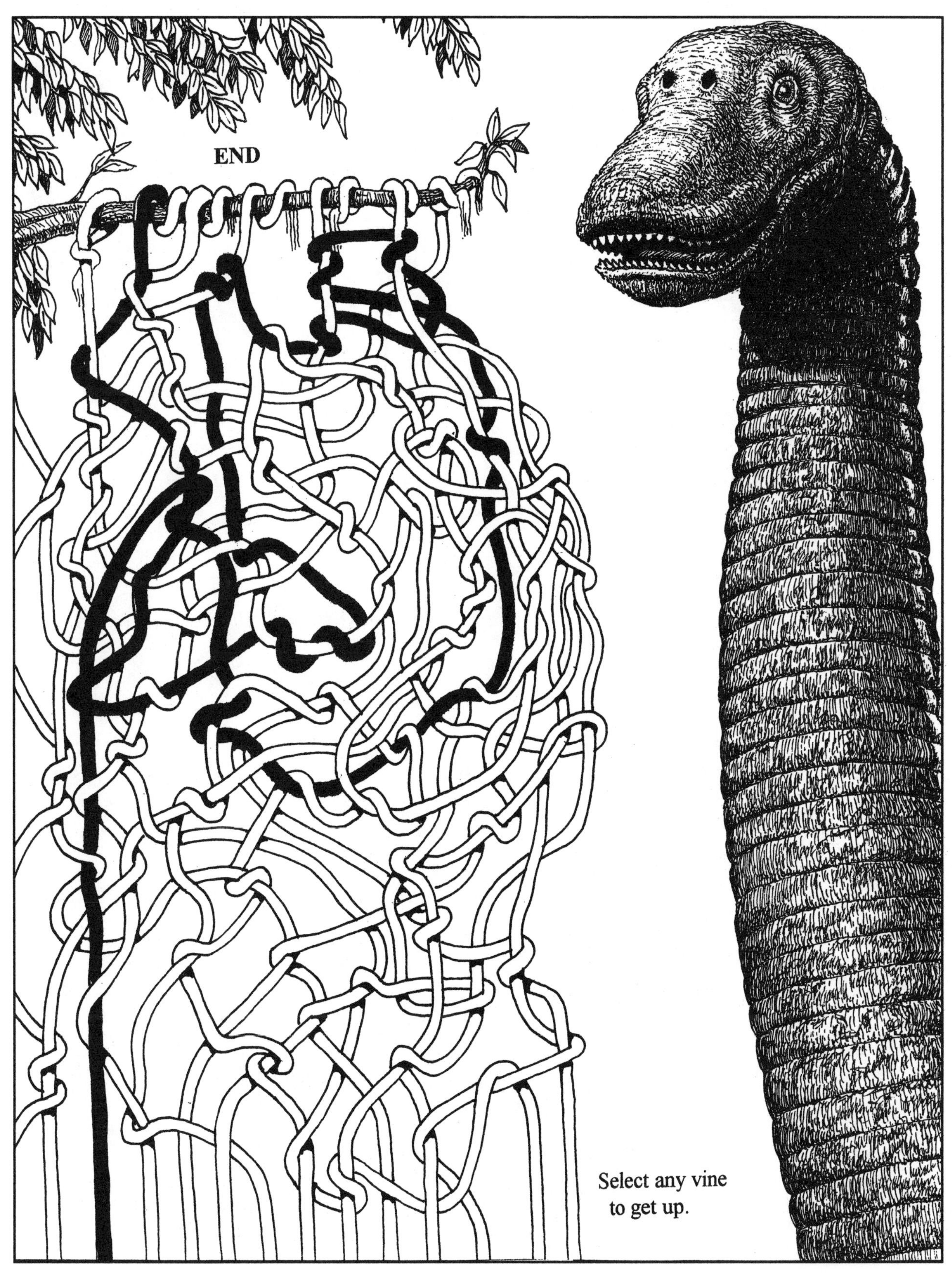

Switch to any vine to get down.
END

END
START

END
START

Retrieve Your Camera

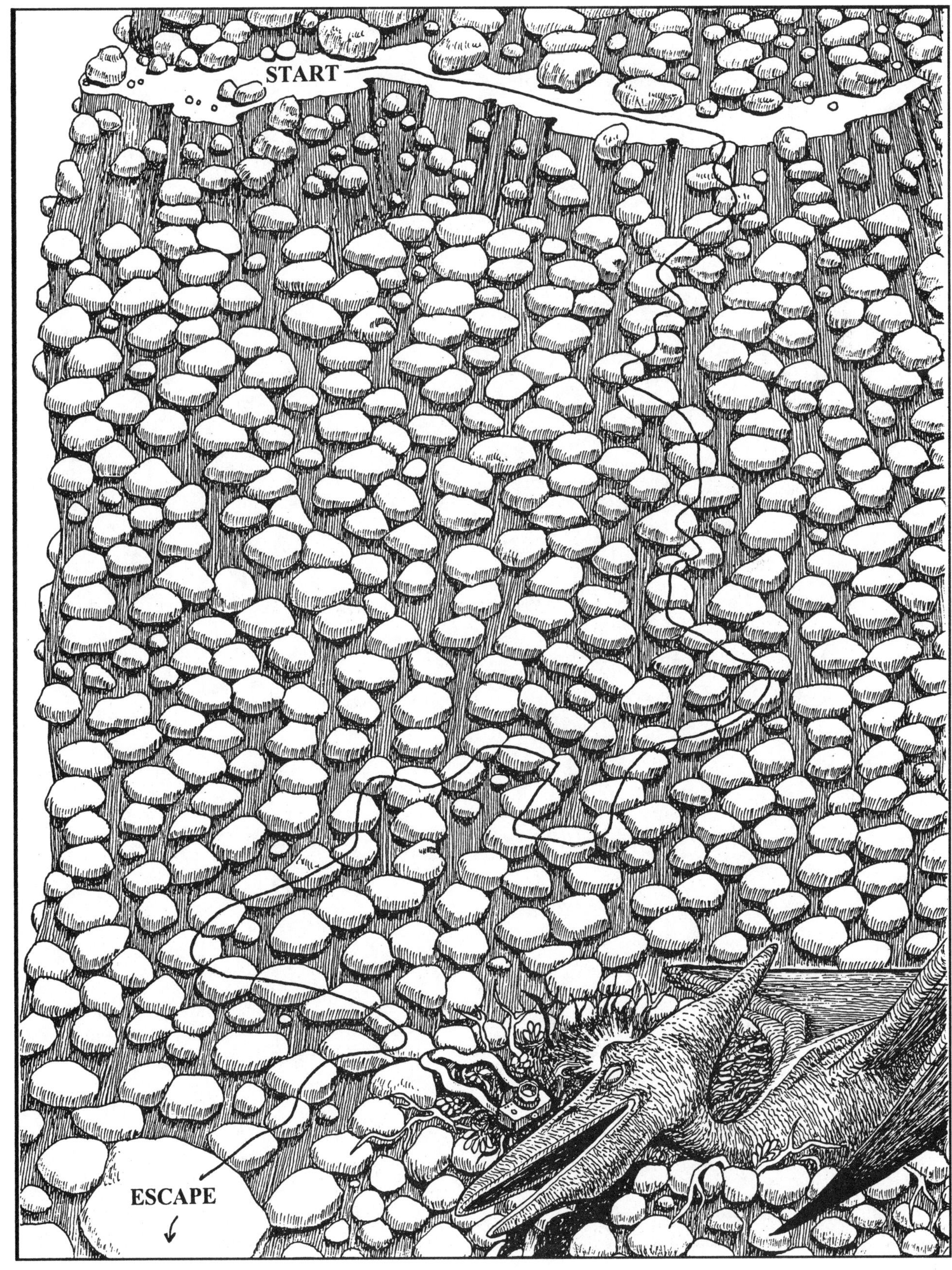

Create a Fossil Bed

START
SAFETY HERE

Volcanic Eruption

START
END

LOST TREASURE MAZES

CONTENTS

Introduction

Stories of lost treasure are not uncommon. Great treasures have been lost throughout history. The loss almost always occurs as a result of unplanned events—from natural disaster to murder—and is usually surrounded by rumor, mystery, and intrigue.

Many treasures lost in the inaccessible depths of the seas have been found and recovered thanks to modern detecting and submersible equipment. On land, metal detectors and sophisticated sonar equipment can help, but the main effort still requires backbreaking hours of research and legwork and often involves great danger. Even when the location of a treasure is known, the conditions for retrieving it are often highly unsafe and the danger is great. Nevertheless, the desire for wealth and the lure of the find can be so great that a few will take the risk and fewer still will occasionally have success. Some become so addicted to the quest that they spend a lifetime searching in vain for that elusive "lost treasure."

Now you have an opportunity to go forth in search of some of the greatest treasures ever lost. As with every hunt for lost treasure, there will be great danger. Don't give up. Your reward, if you are successful, will be beyond your wildest dreams.

The Trail to King John's Castle

You are going to try and find the lost crown jewels of King John of England. Start down this trail on your way to his castle. Find a clear path.

The Courtyard

Cross through the courtyard to the castle. Enter at any one of the doors on the far side.

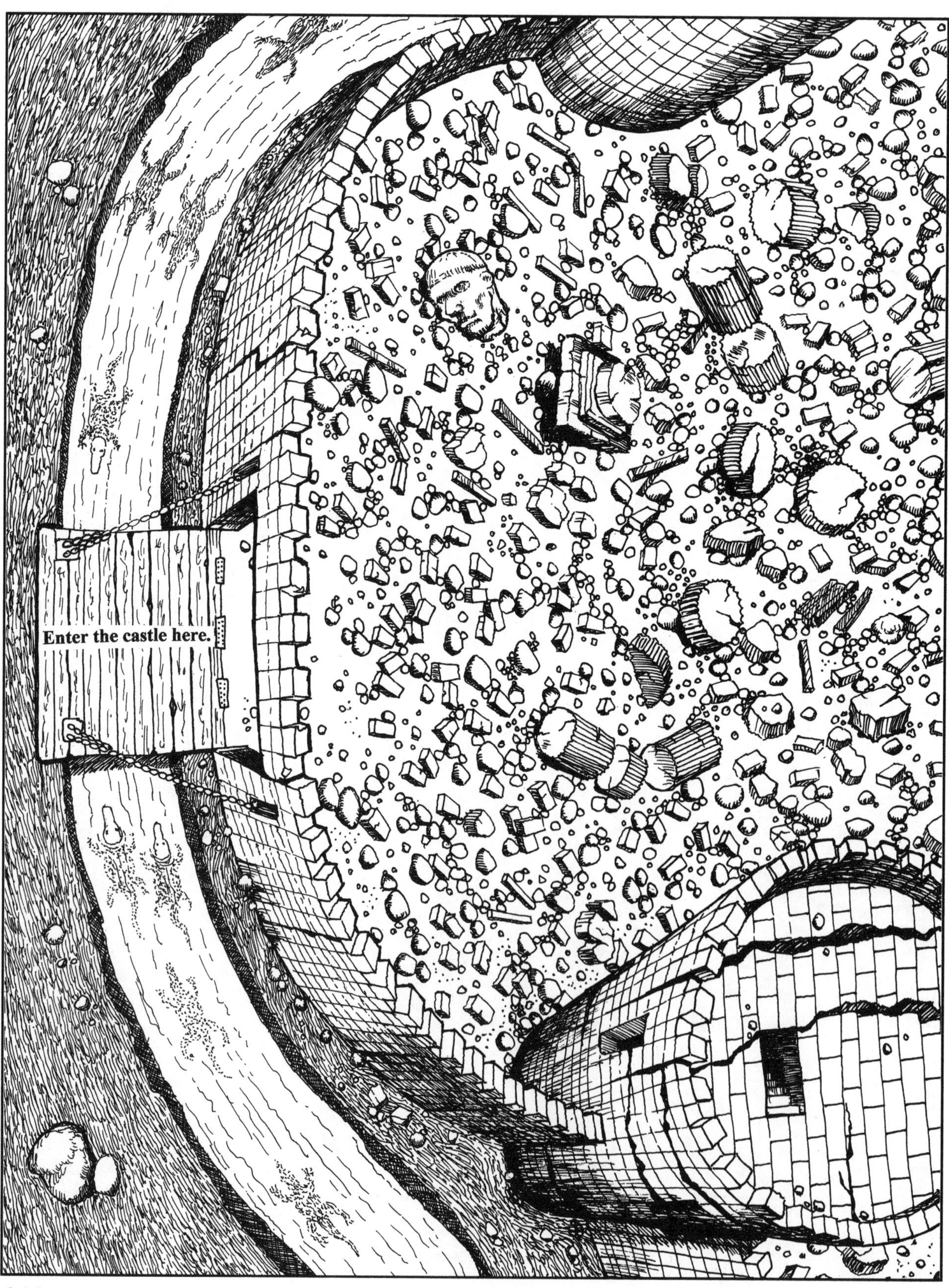

Continue through one of these doors.

The Banquet Room

Cross through the banquet room without disturbing anything. Move into the next room through one of the three doors.

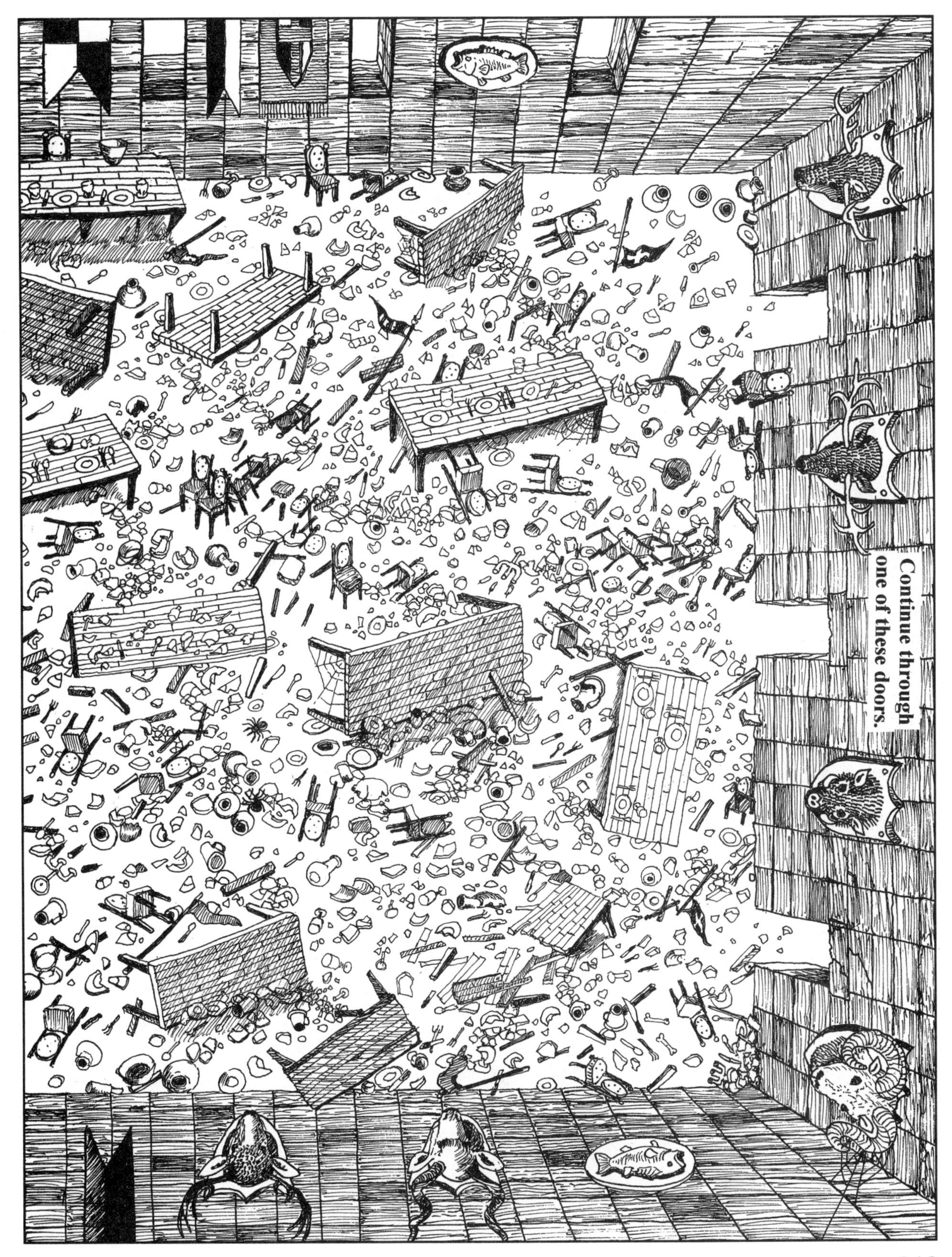
Continue through one of these doors.

King John's Throne Room

Many treasure robbers have tried to get to the treasure, which is guarded by brave knights. They have failed. Can you succeed? Find a clear path.

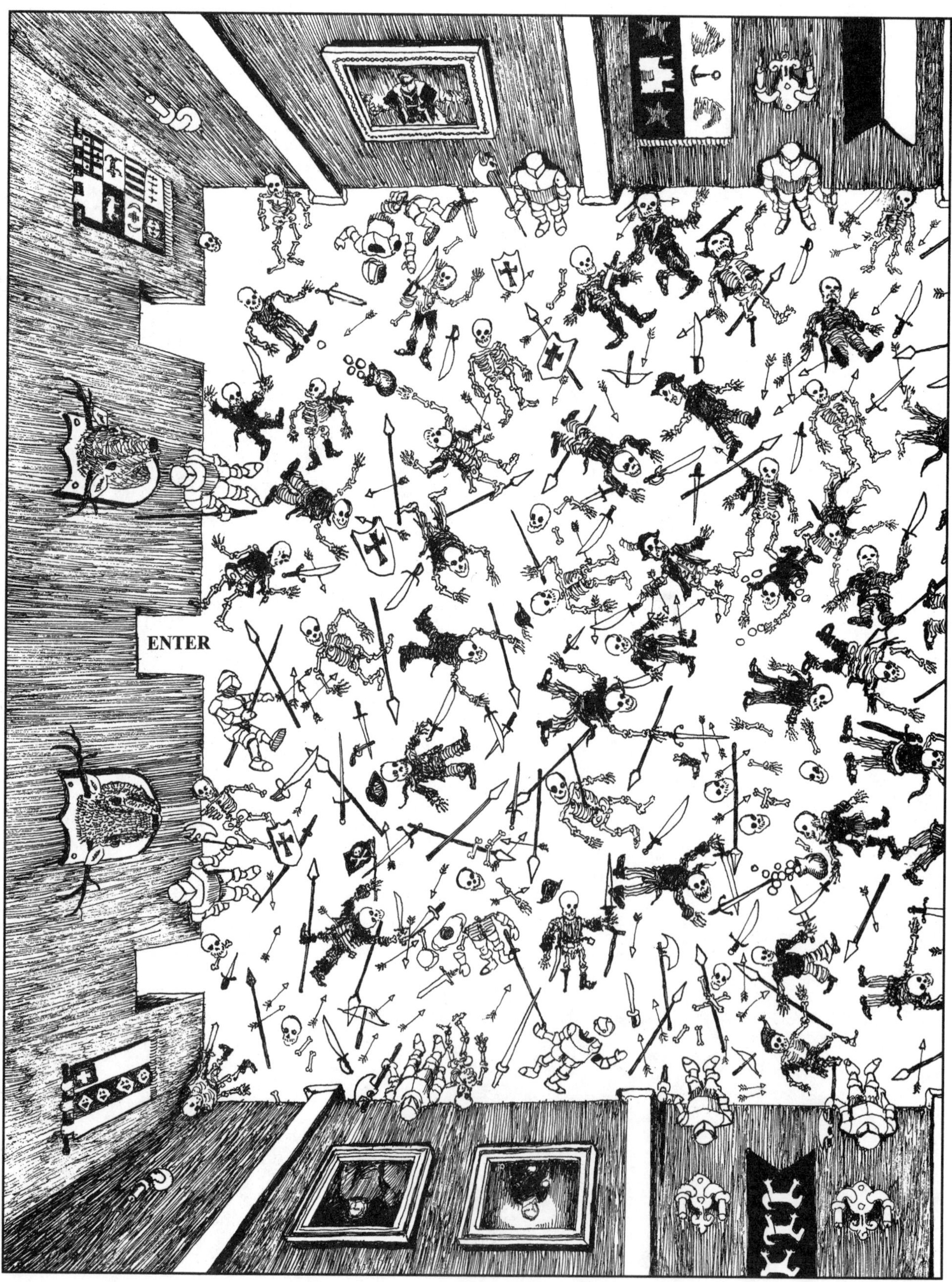

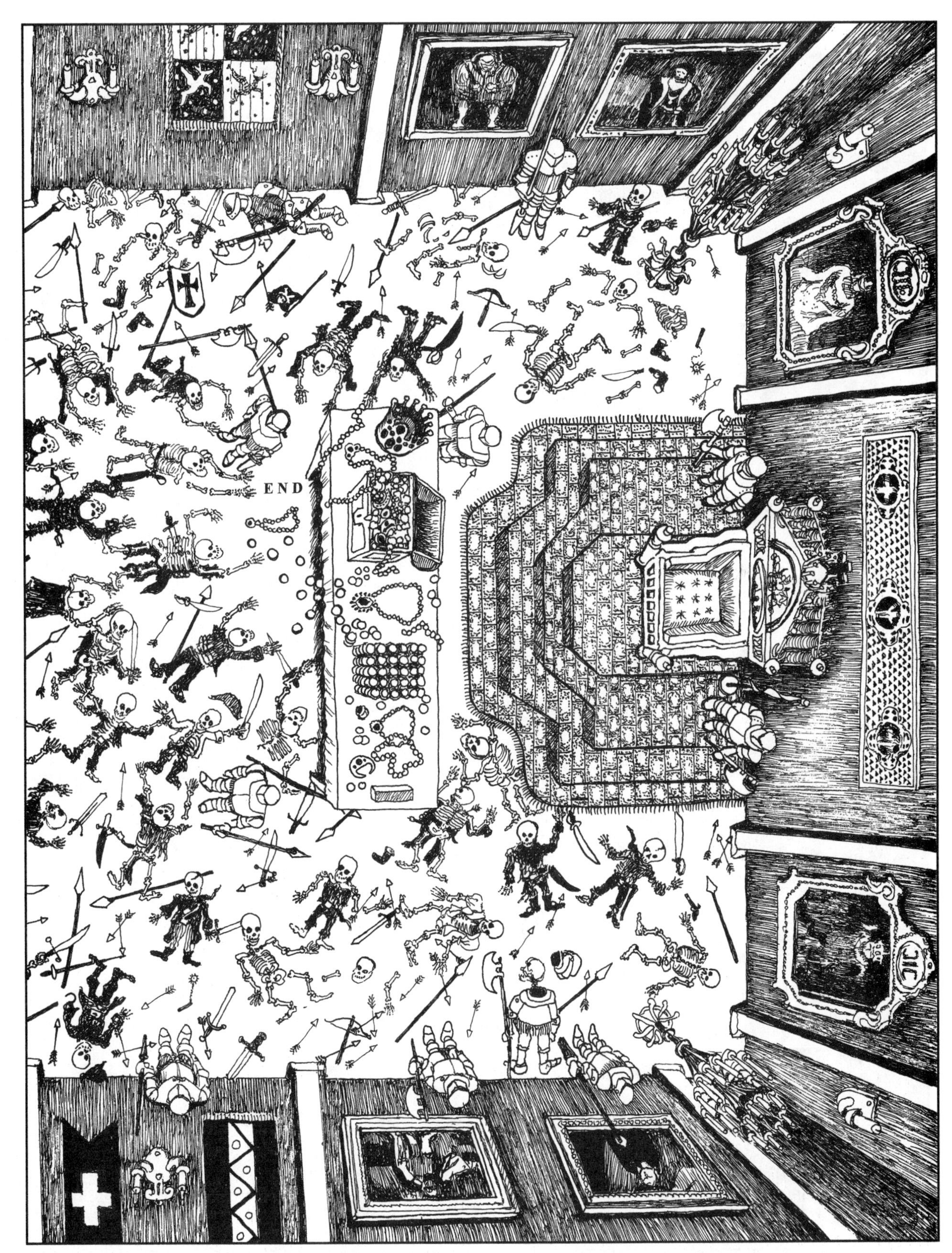
END

S.S. *Central America*

In 1857, the side-wheeler S.S. *Central America* sank off the coast of Carolina in a

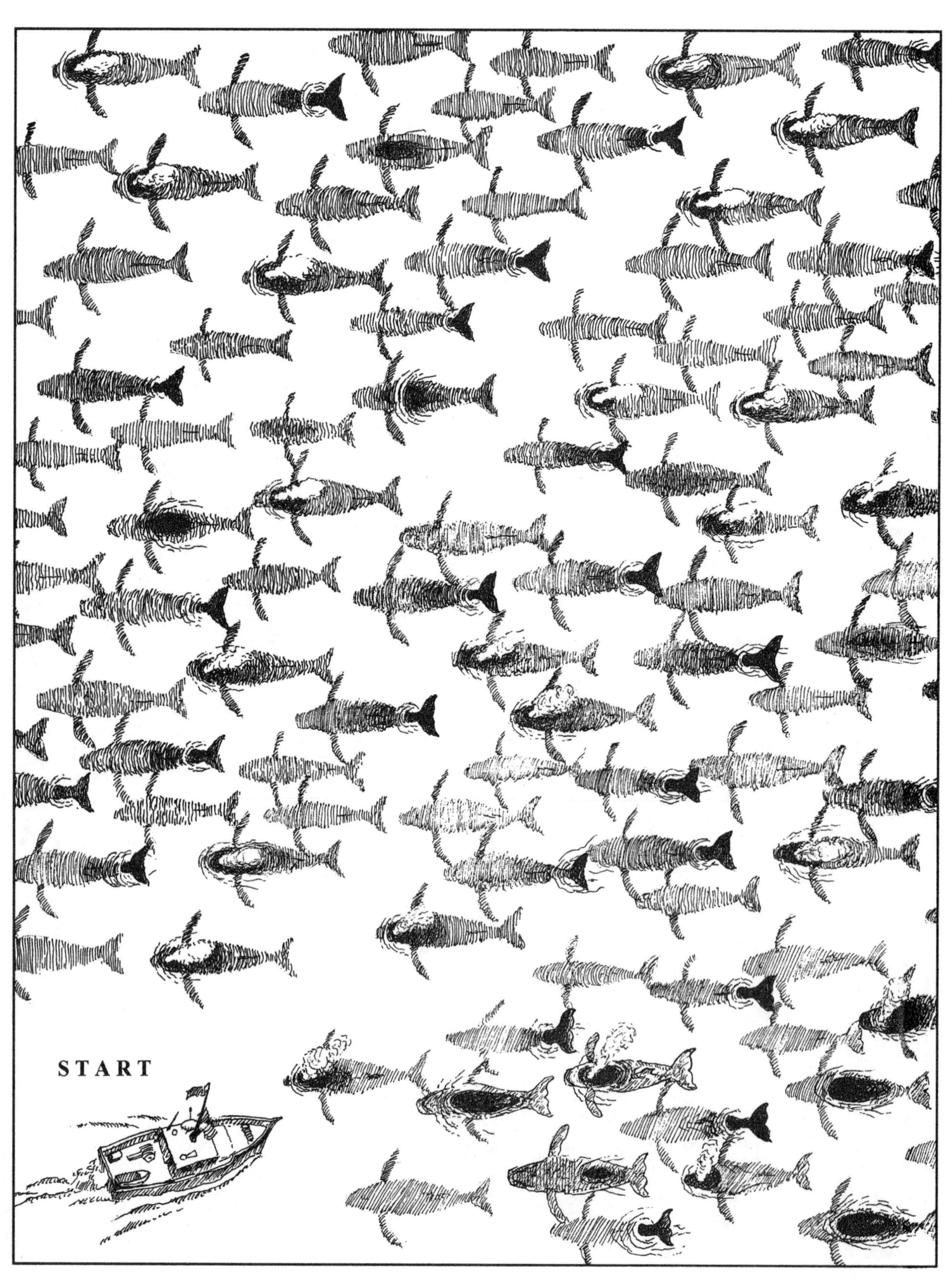

terrible hurricane with perhaps a billion dollars in gold on board. In 1985, this treasure was found and recovered. See if you have the skills to find the *Central America*. Stay clear of the migrating herd of whales and find your way to the ship.

The *Concepcion's* Treasure

You have found the *Concepcion* and you know from the ship's logs from hundreds

of years ago that there is great treasure, Spanish *reales* and silver bars, to be recovered. However, in order to salvage the treasure you must avoid the dangerous sea life of the reef and find a clear route to the remains of the ship.

The Treasure of Pinaki Atoll

In the early 1880's, four Australian mercenaries buried a great treasure stolen

from Peru on Pinaki Atoll. To this day it is still missing, and some believe it was located and dumped at sea to avoid a curse. Can you find a clear path to the treasure without disturbing the local sea life and then escape?

The Money Pit 1

This treasure was buried at the bottom of a deep sand pit. As you dig your way to the treasure, retrieve the coins as you go. You can go down and cross over into another pit, but you can not go up. Total your coins when you get to the bottom.

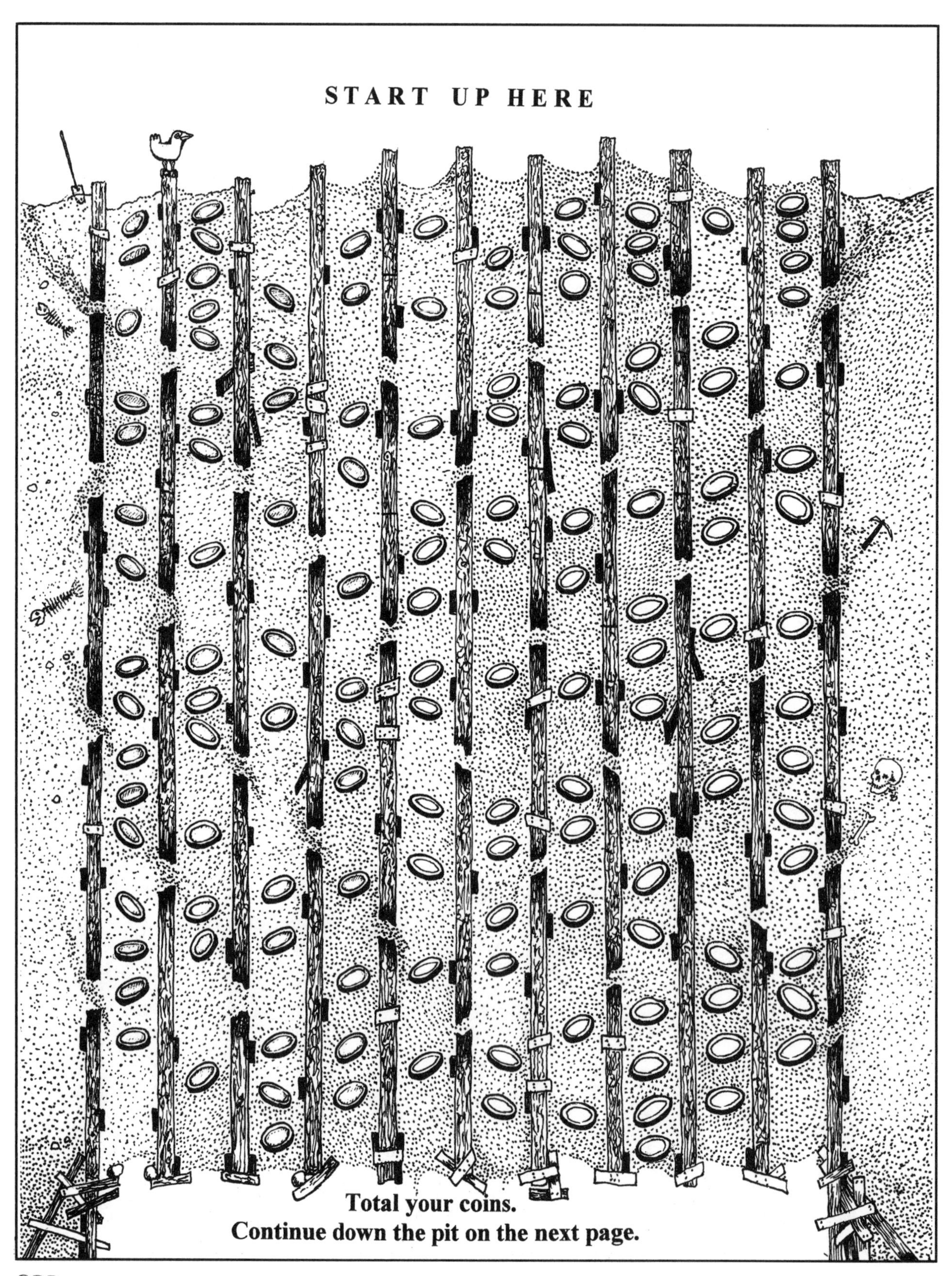

The Money Pit 2

Continue down the pit starting at the top according to the number of coins you collected in pit 1. The same rules apply as in pit 1. You must have exactly 35 coins in order to obtain the key to open the treasure chests. Good luck.

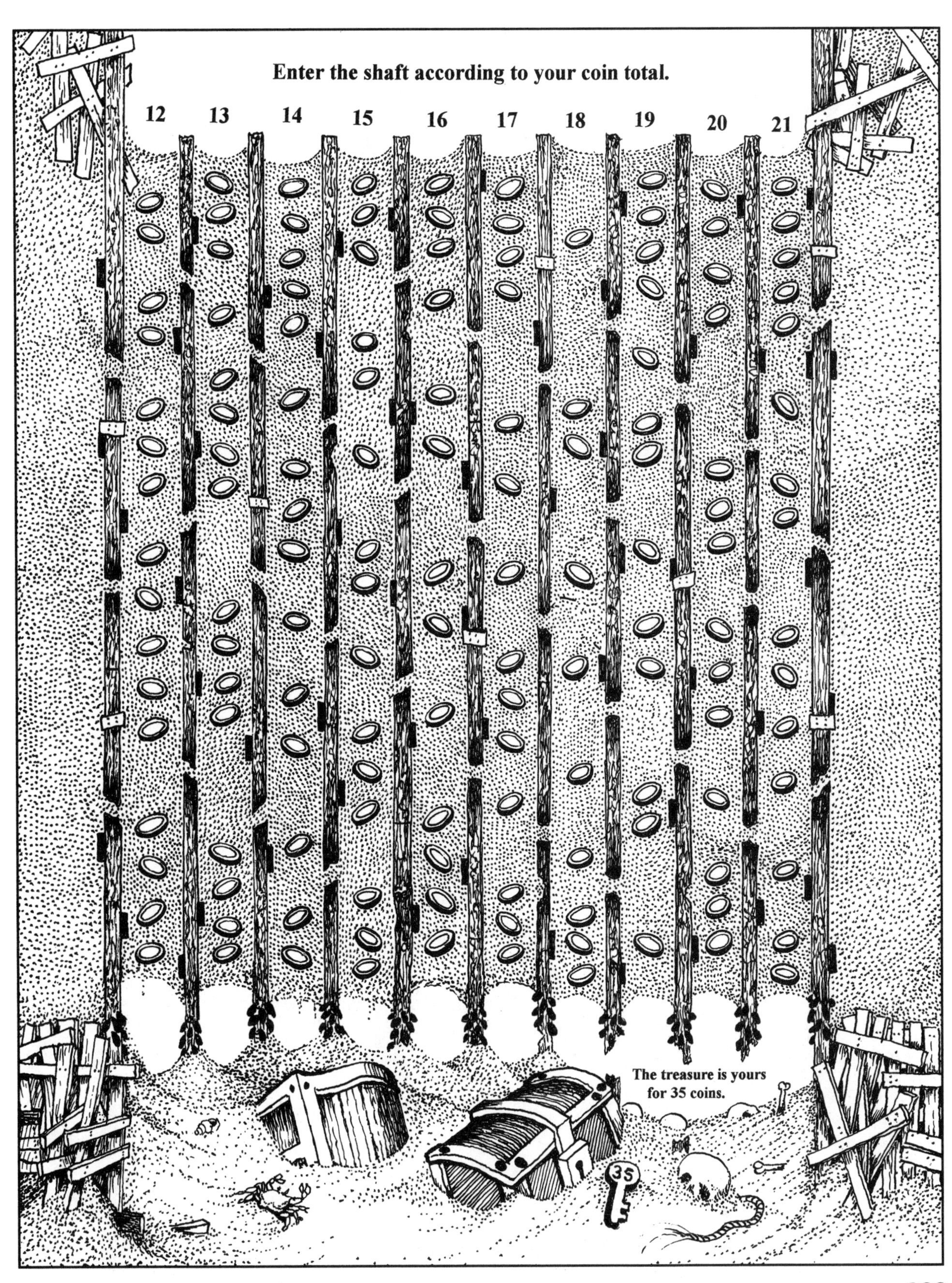

The Lost Dutchman Mine

The Lost Dutchman Mine is situated in the Superstition Mountains, 40 miles from

Phoenix, Arizona. Over the last century, many have travelled through sacred Indian land, into the mountains to find the mine and have never come out. Can you find a clear trail to the mine? Be careful. This is a dangerous quest.

Victorio Peak

The treasure of Emperor Maximilian of Mexico, thousands of bars of gold stacked

like cordwood along with 27 human skeletons, was found in a cave on Victorio Peak in New Mexico. When the entrance caved in, the treasure was lost. Find your way to Maximilian's gold by finding a clear passageway.

Sutro's Tunnel

The mines beneath Virginia City have filled with water. A lot of silver can still be

mined if the water can be drained. From 1869 to 1878, Adolph Sutro's crew dug a tunnel 4 miles under Virginia City to drain the mines, but now it is plugged. Swim down and blast away the plug.

The Trek

Out there, somewhere in the jungles of Central America, is a lost Mayan Temple.

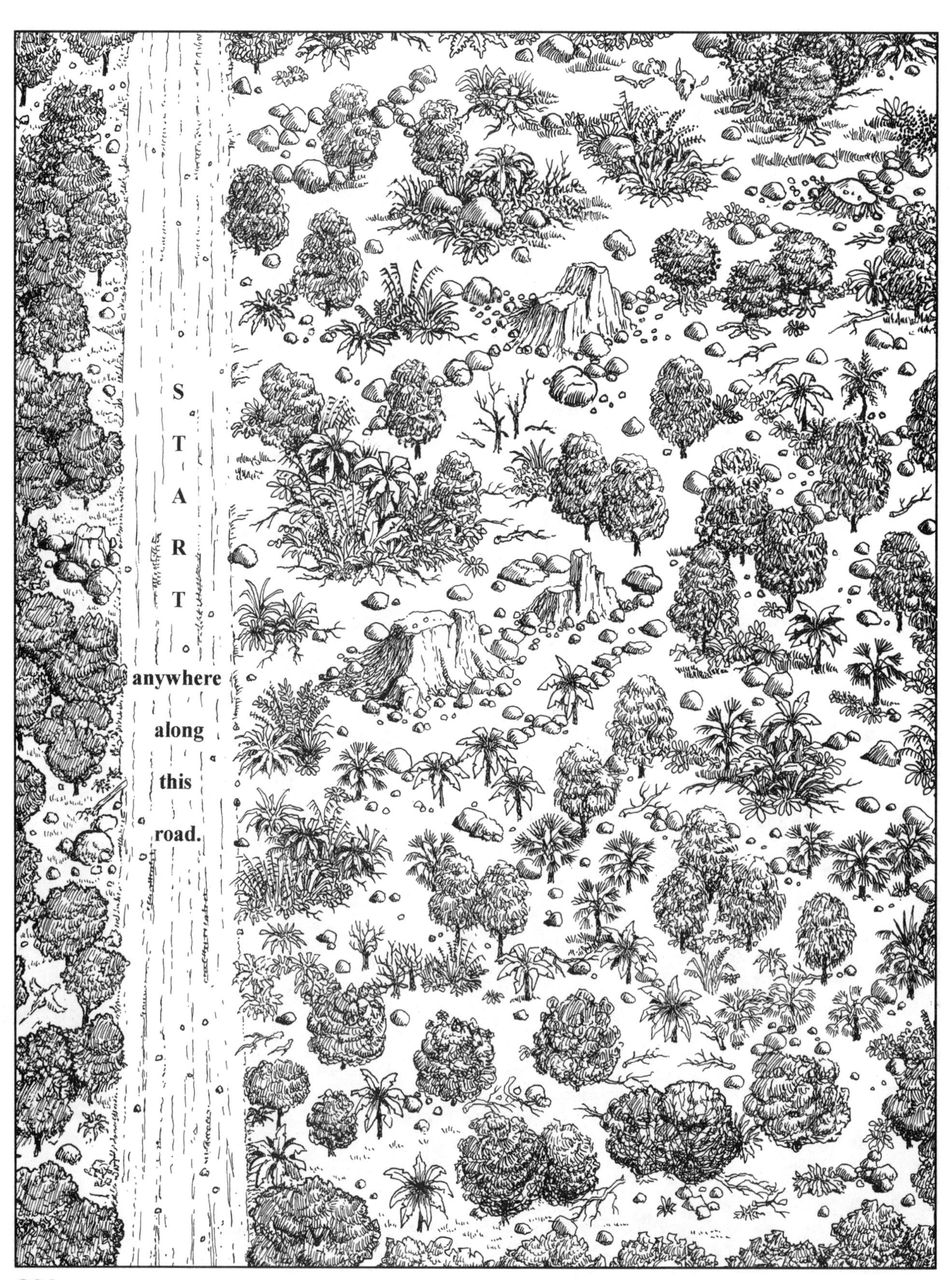

A search can be dangerous and take many days. Begin your trek to the right of the dirt road. You must find a clear path going east.

The Ruins

Find your way through these ancient ruins to the temple steps ahead.

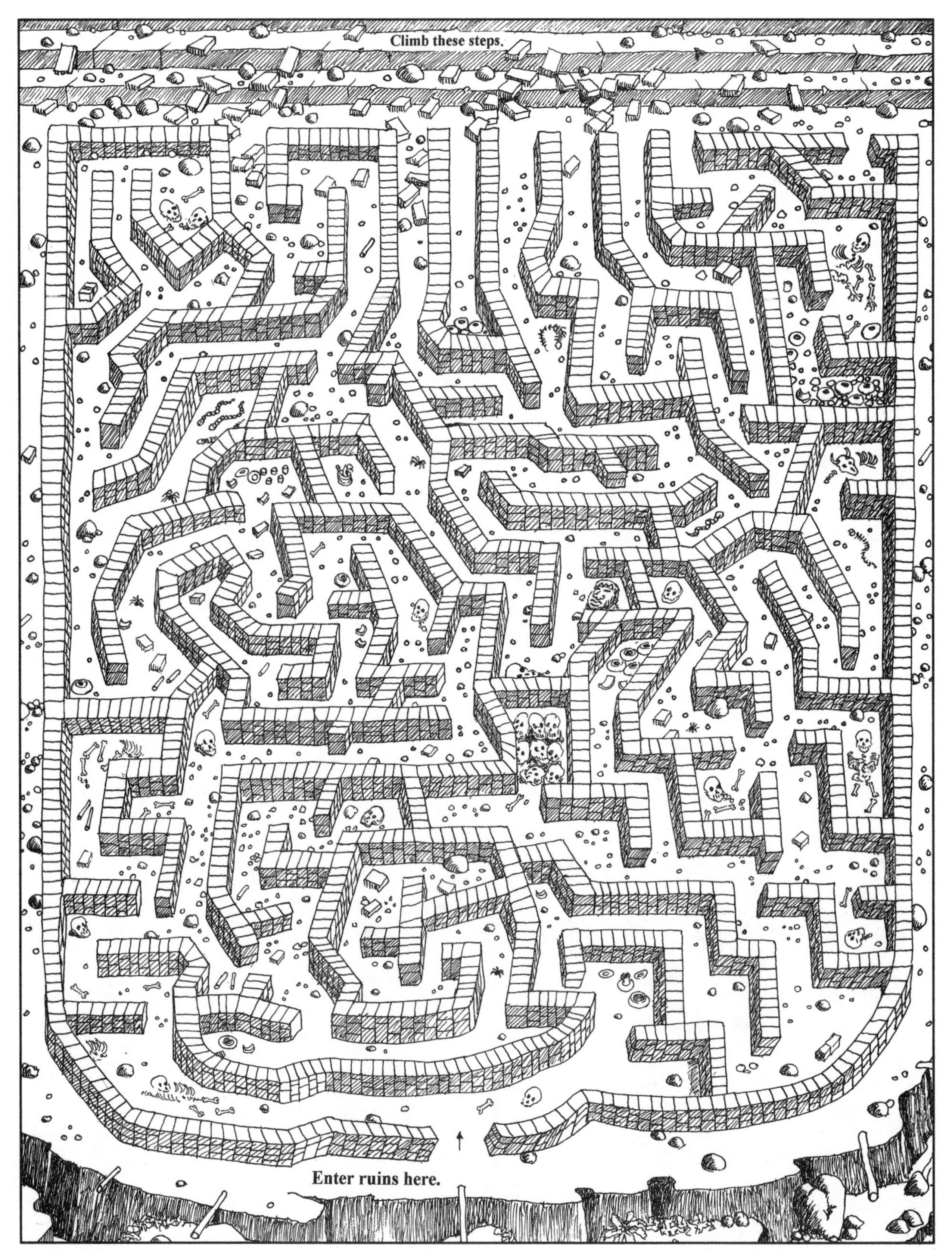

The Lost Mayan Temple

You must pick your way across the ruins to reach the steps of the temple before you. Find a clear path.

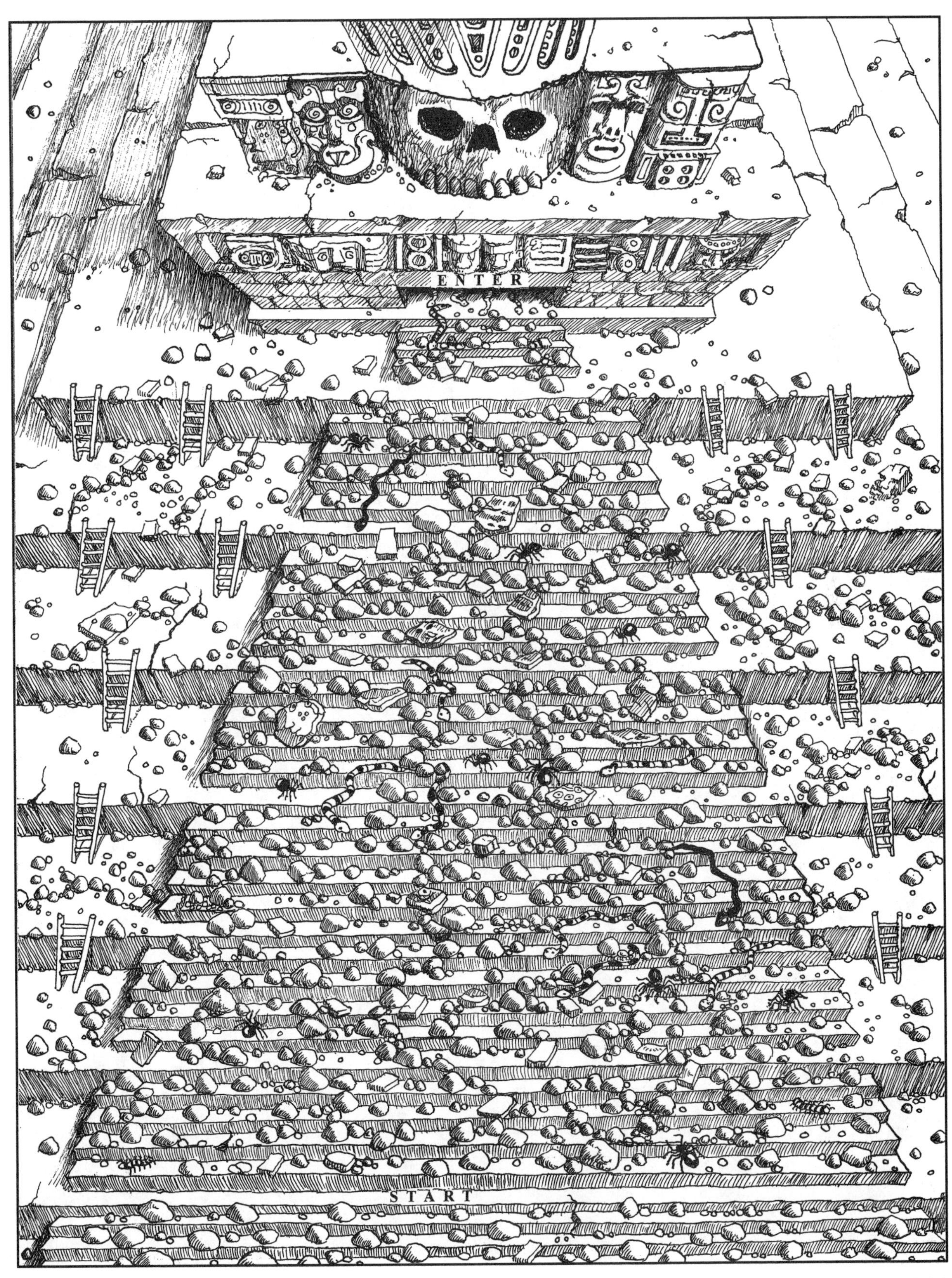

Oh No, Snakes

You must stay clear of all the snakes to reach the door at the top of the temple stairs.

THIS WAY...

The Gold Idol

This looks easy. Up ahead there seems to be a gold idol for the taking. But wait!

Notice that every dark tile is a trap door. Do not step on a dark tile and do not move at an angle—right and left turns only. If you reach the idol, you still must find your way out through one of the 13 remaining doors.

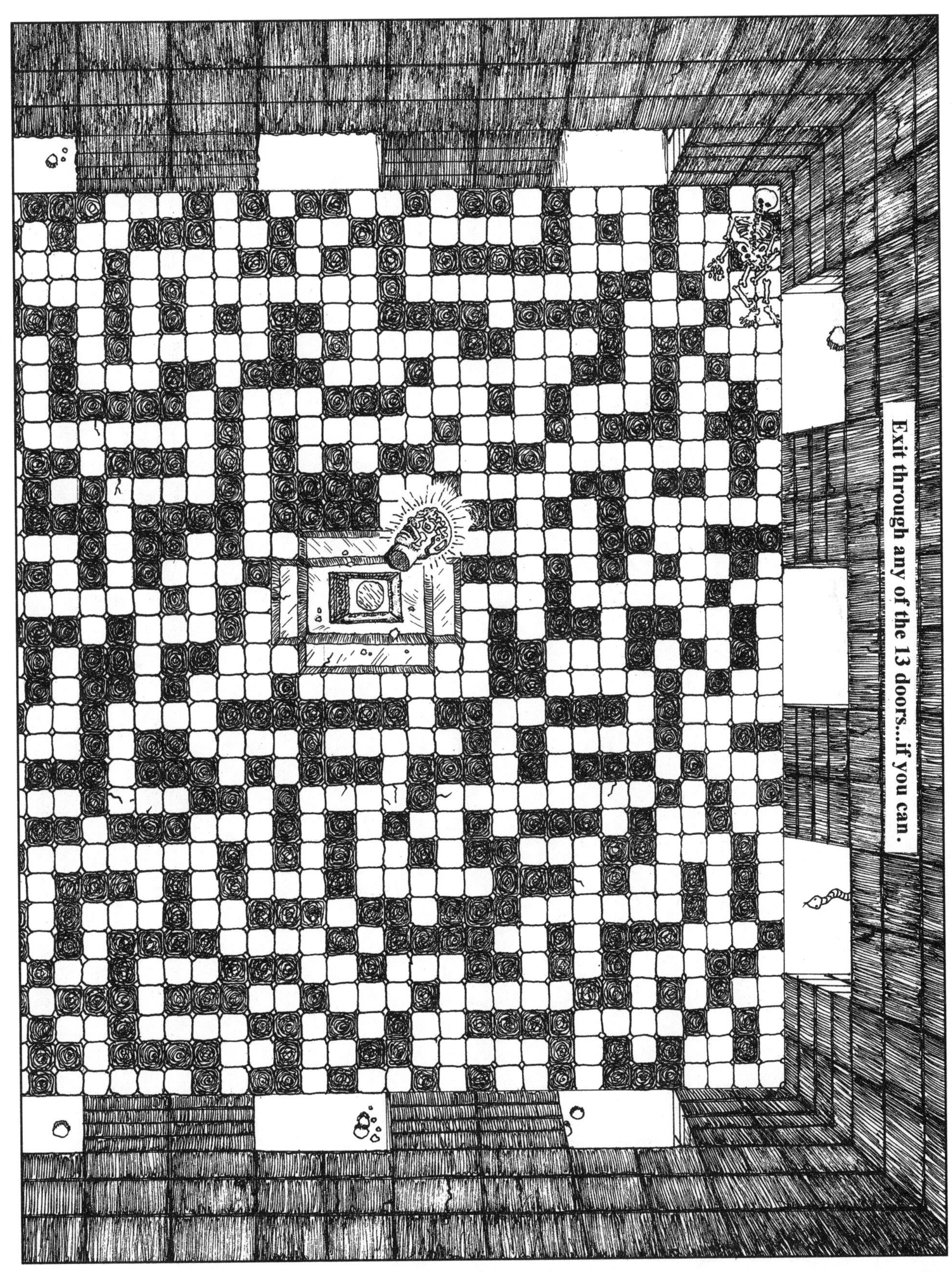

CONGRATULATIONS

Finding lost treasure has never been easy, as you know. The keys to your success in these quests have been your courage, perseverance and dogged determination. Your rewards for these character traits have been great.

With the vast wealth that you now possess, your new challenge will be how to use it wisely. You will discover that using it for your own needs and self-indulgence will not bring you happiness or fulfillment. Certainly, you deserve some comforts, but only as you help others, in a world where great suffering occurs, will you experience real lasting joy.

May the world be a better place as a product of your thoughtfulness.

Treasure Guides

If you had any trouble finding your way through the mazes in this section, use the treasure guides on the following pages. Do not use the guides to gain a treasure unfairly. Below is a guide for the cover maze.

The Trail to King John's Castle

The Courtyard

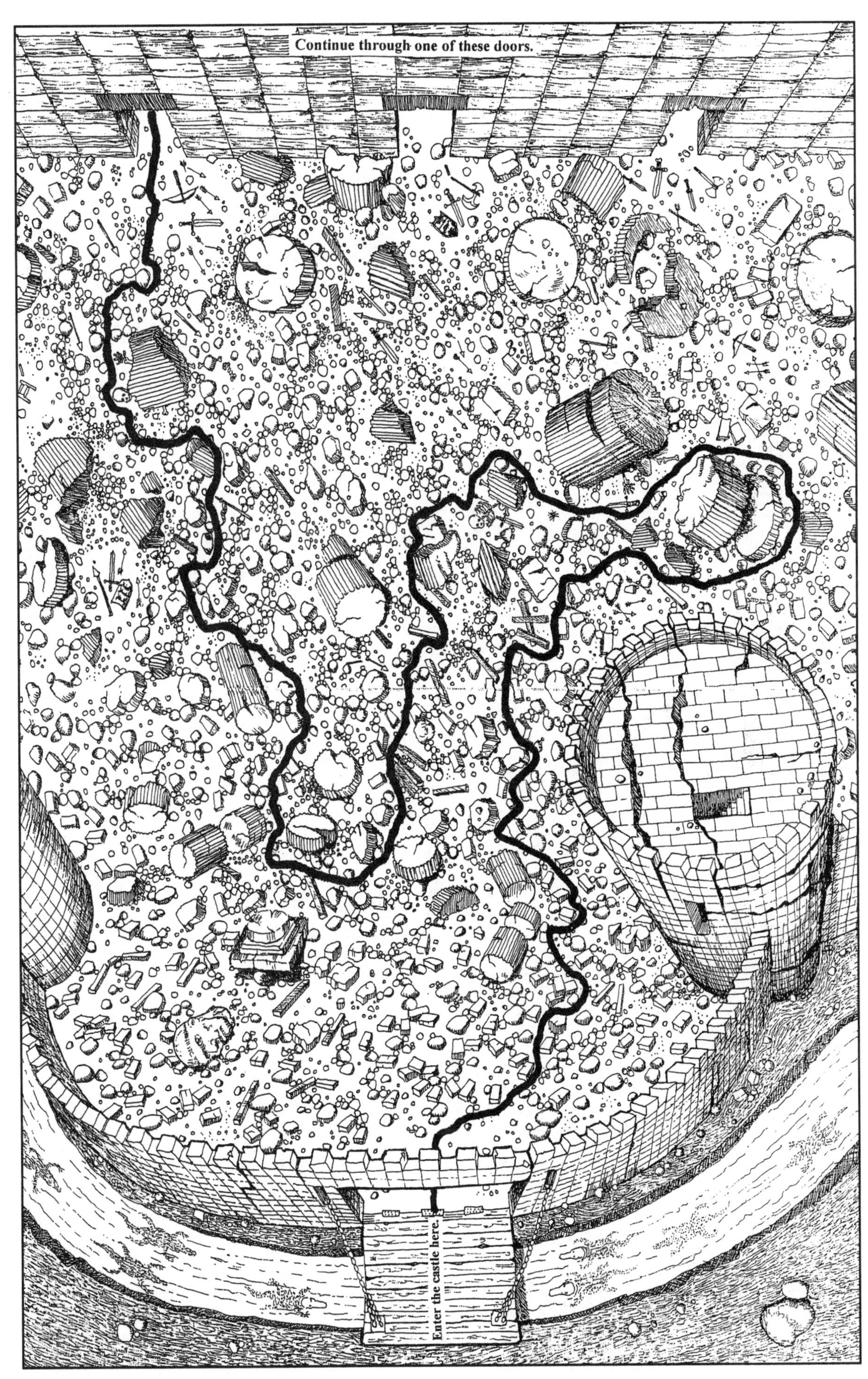

The Banquet Room

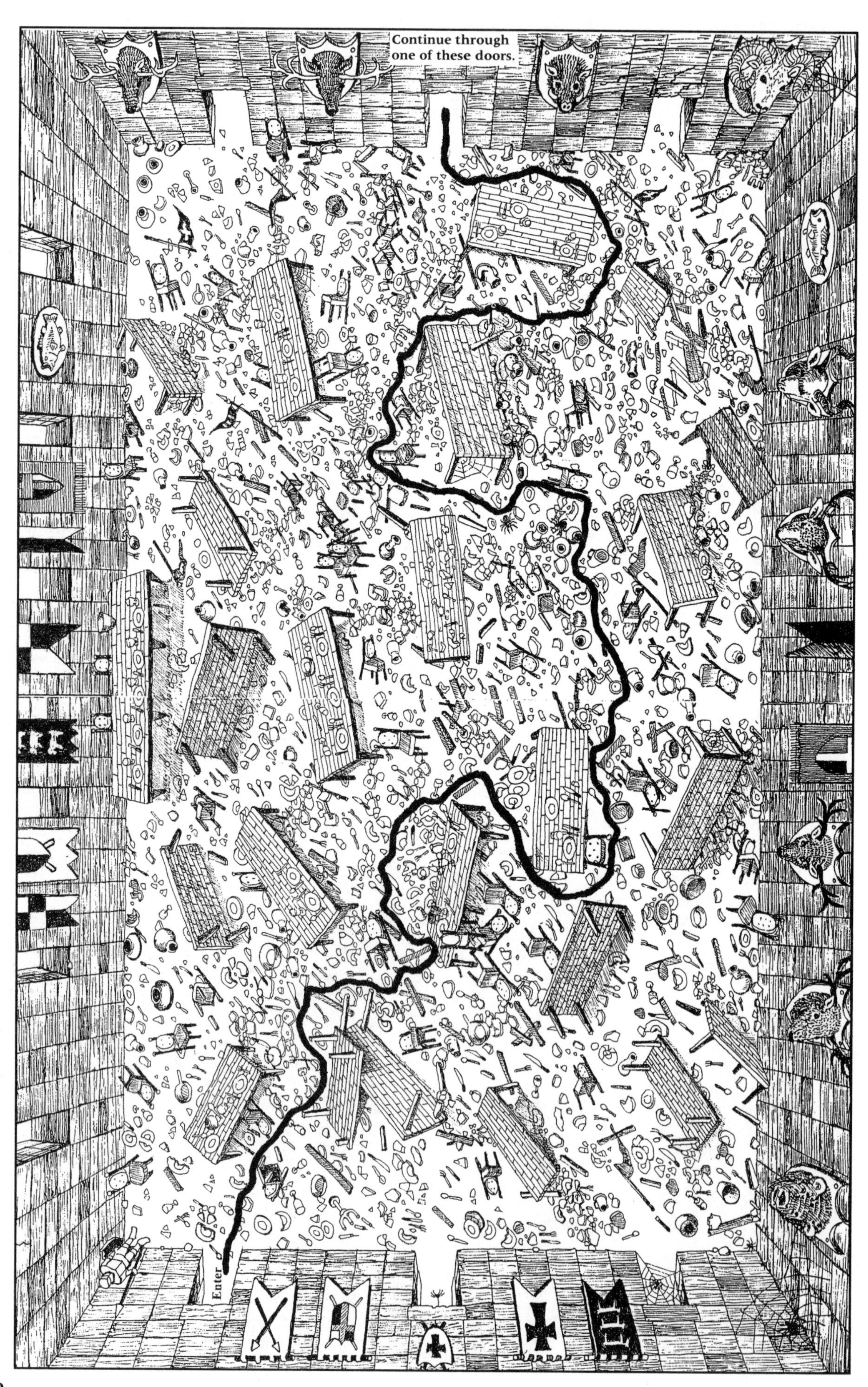

King John's Throne Room

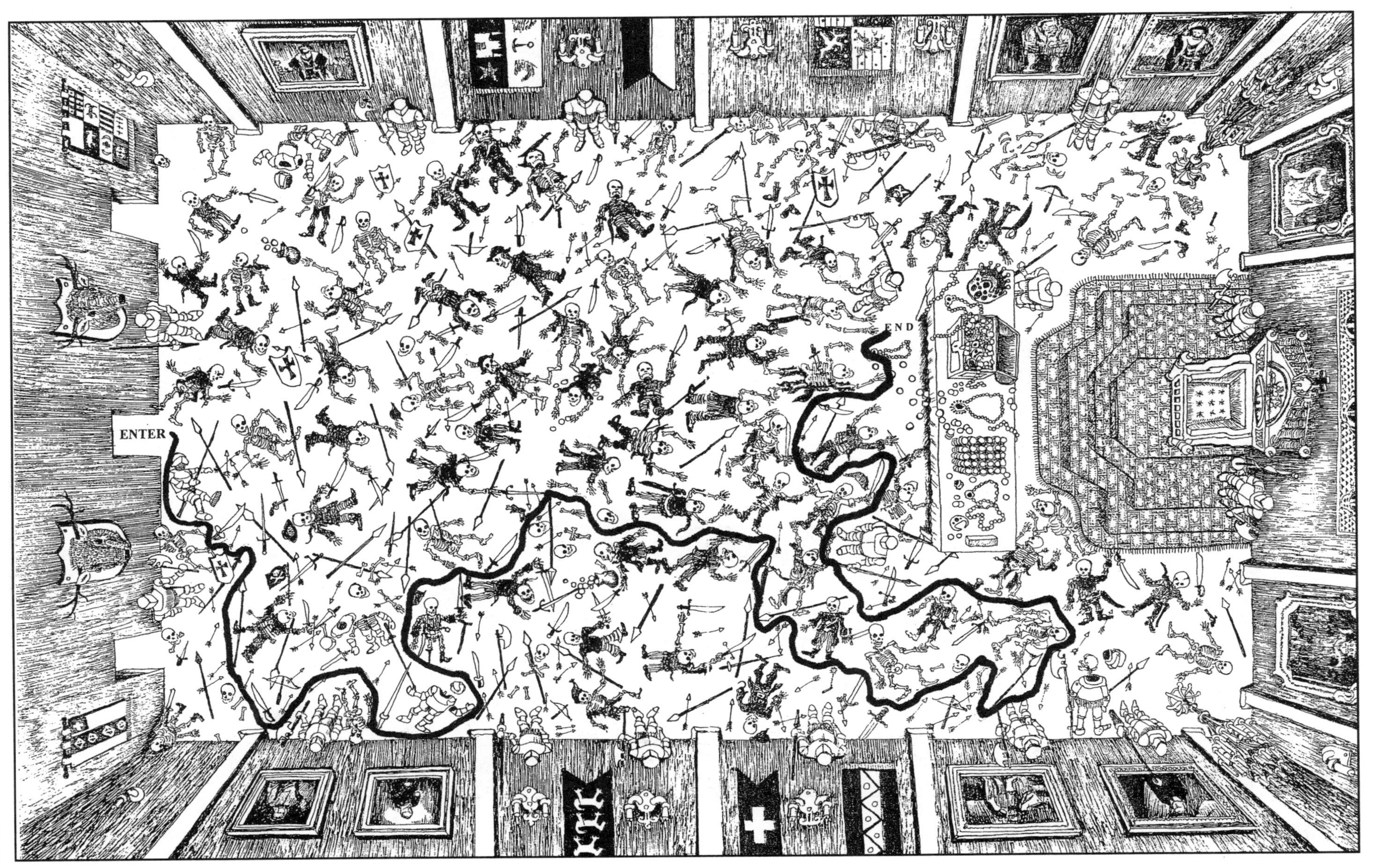

S.S. *Central America*

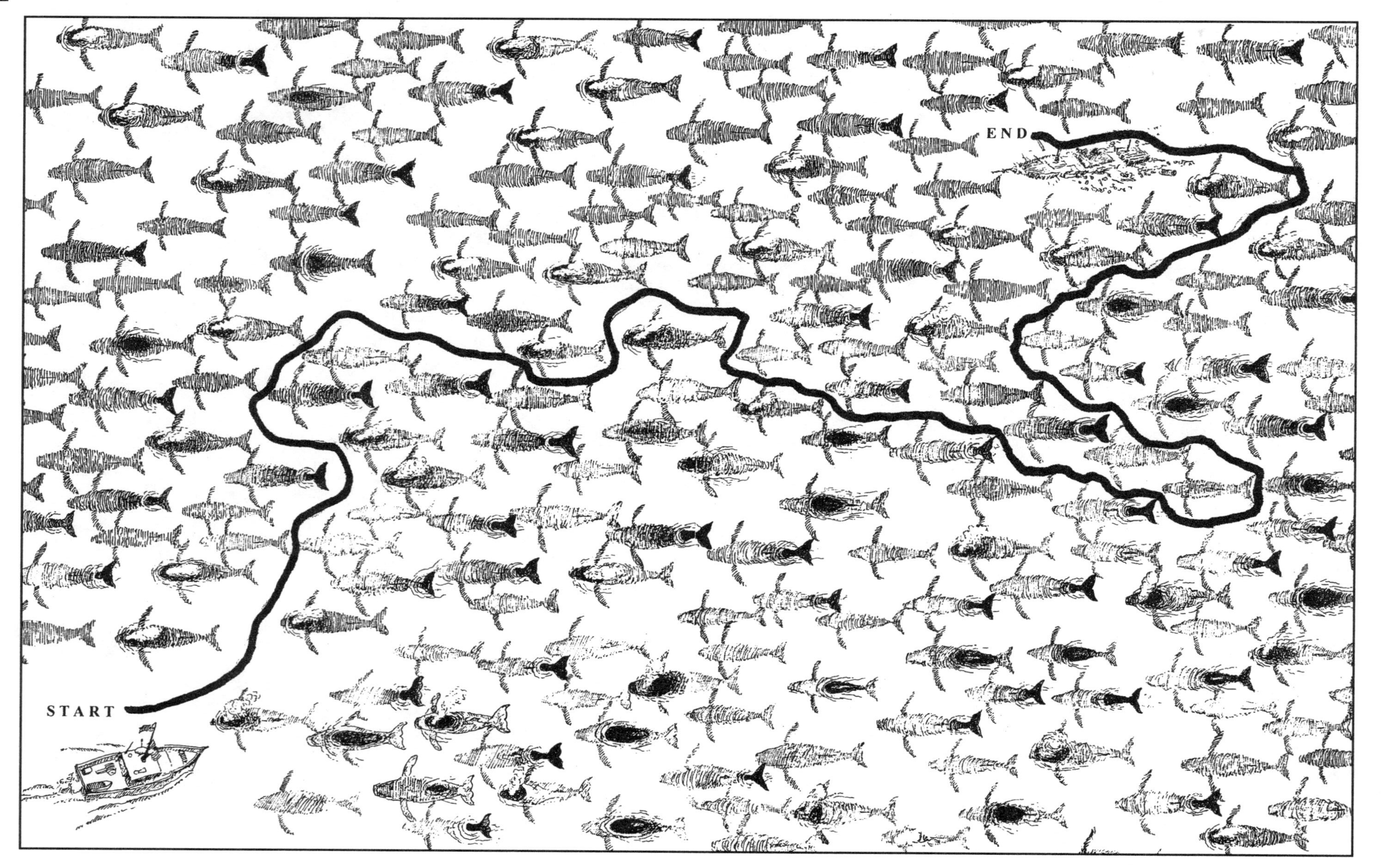

The *Concepcion's* Treasure

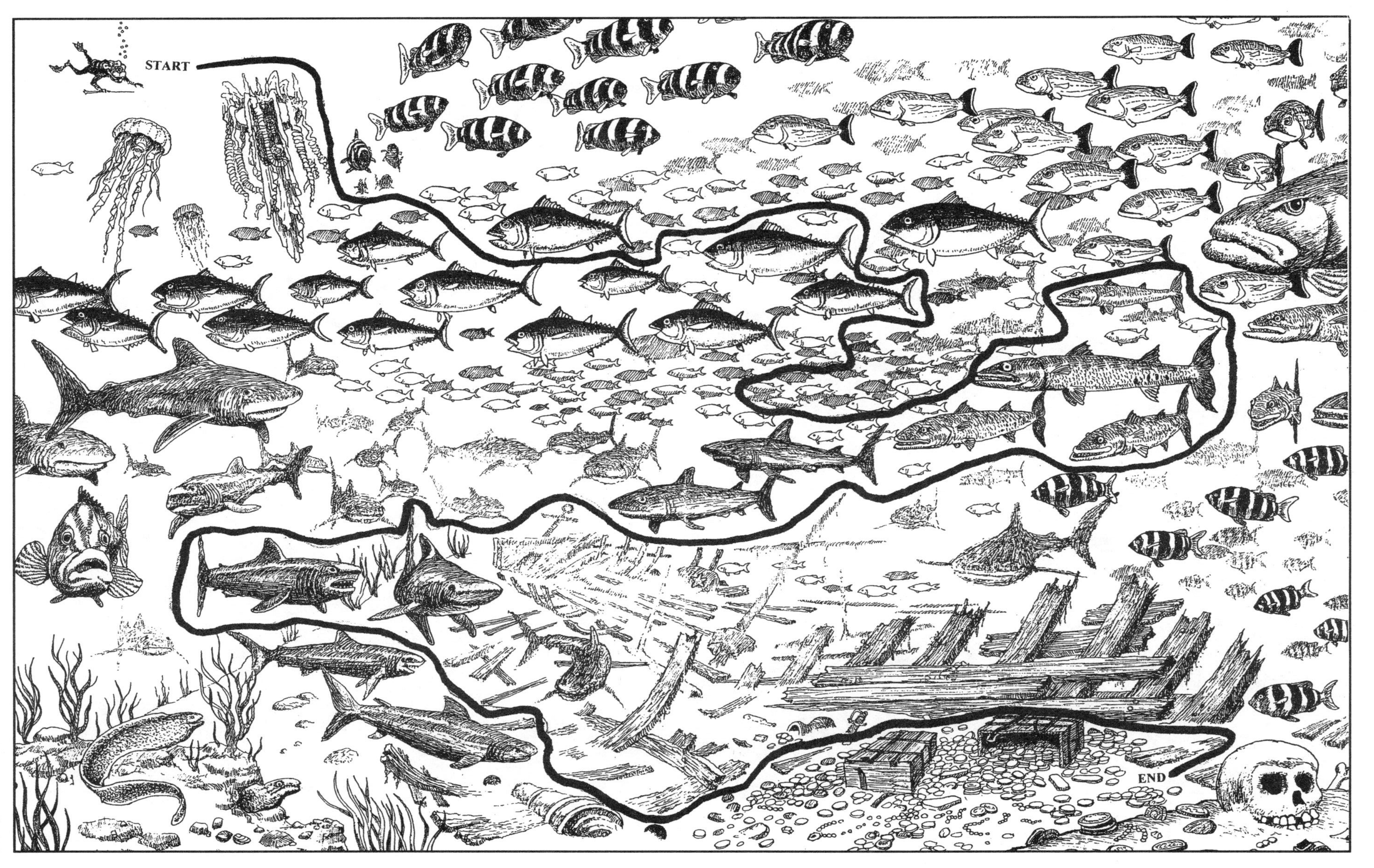

The Treasure of Pinaki Atoll

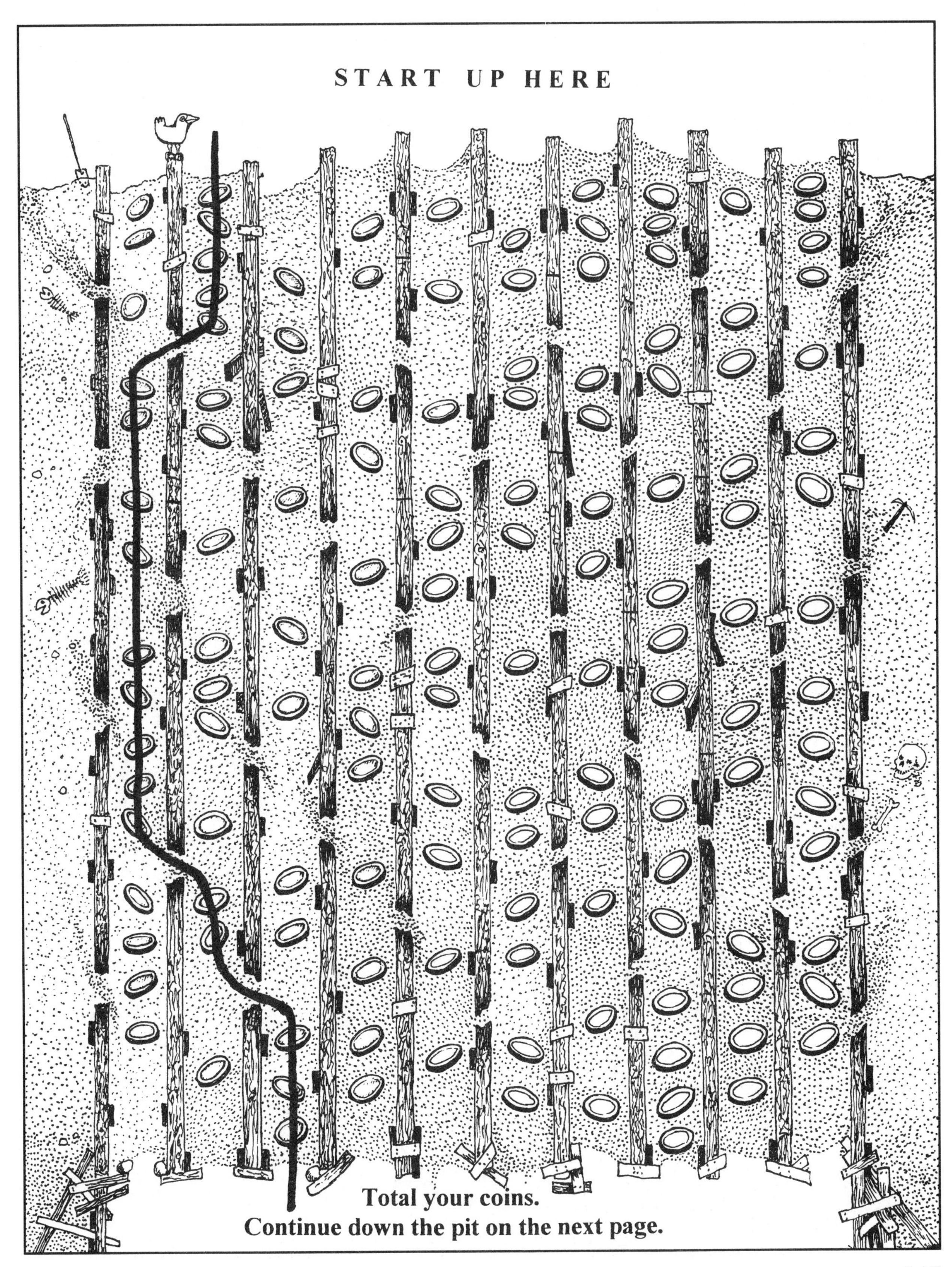
START UP HERE
Total your coins.
Continue down the pit on the next page.

The Money Pit 2

The Lost Dutchman Mine

Victorio Peak

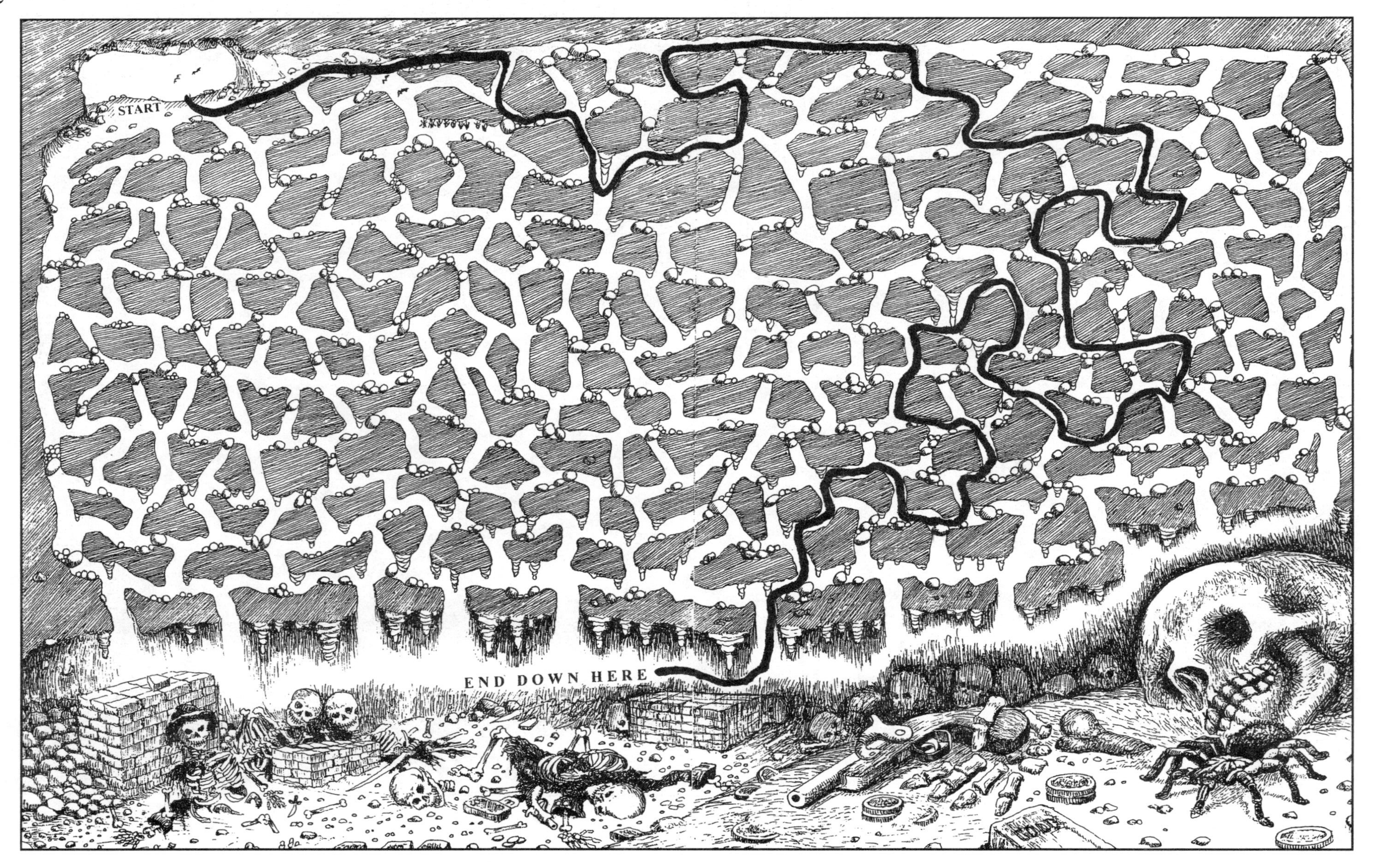

Sutro's Tunnel

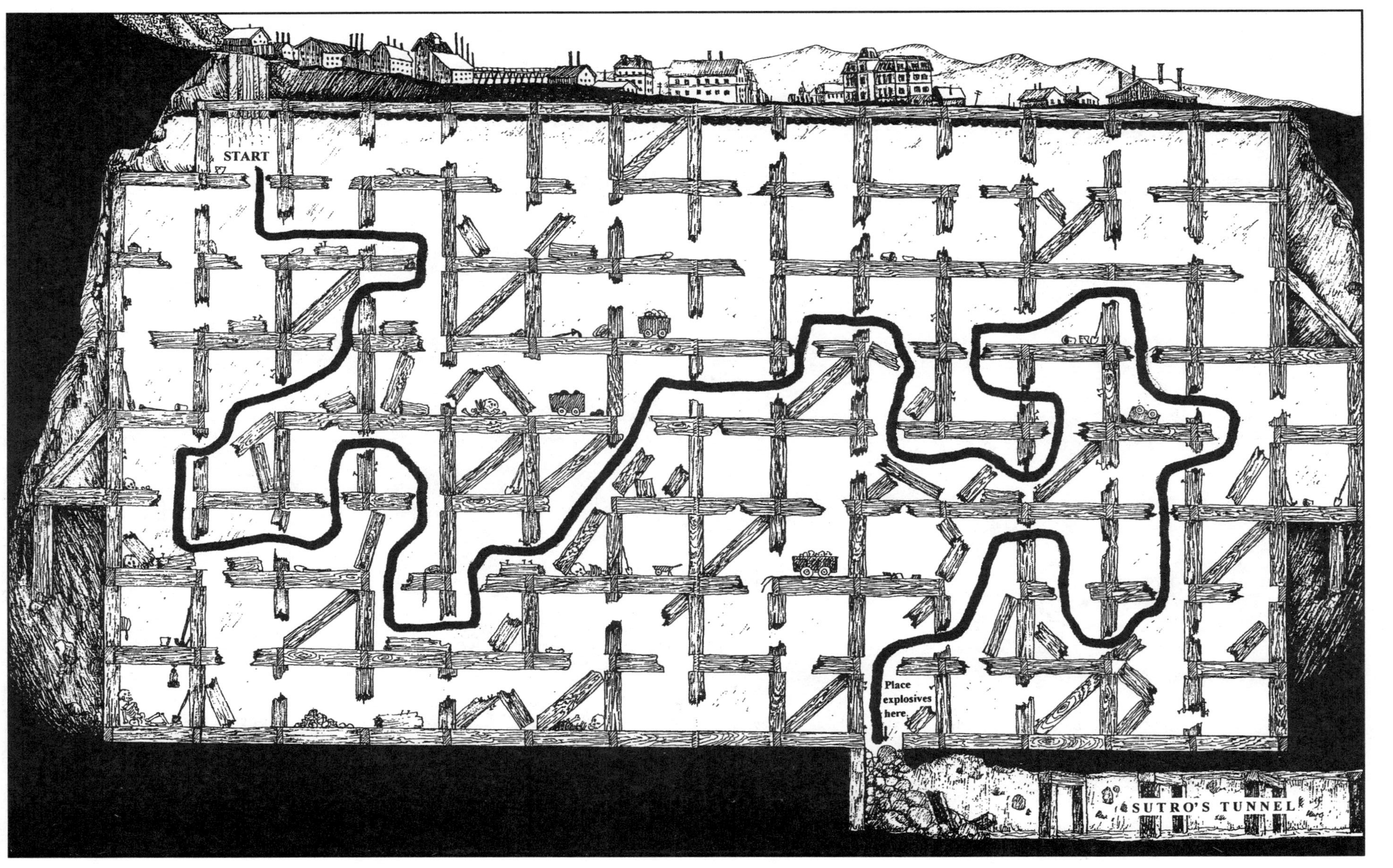

The Trek

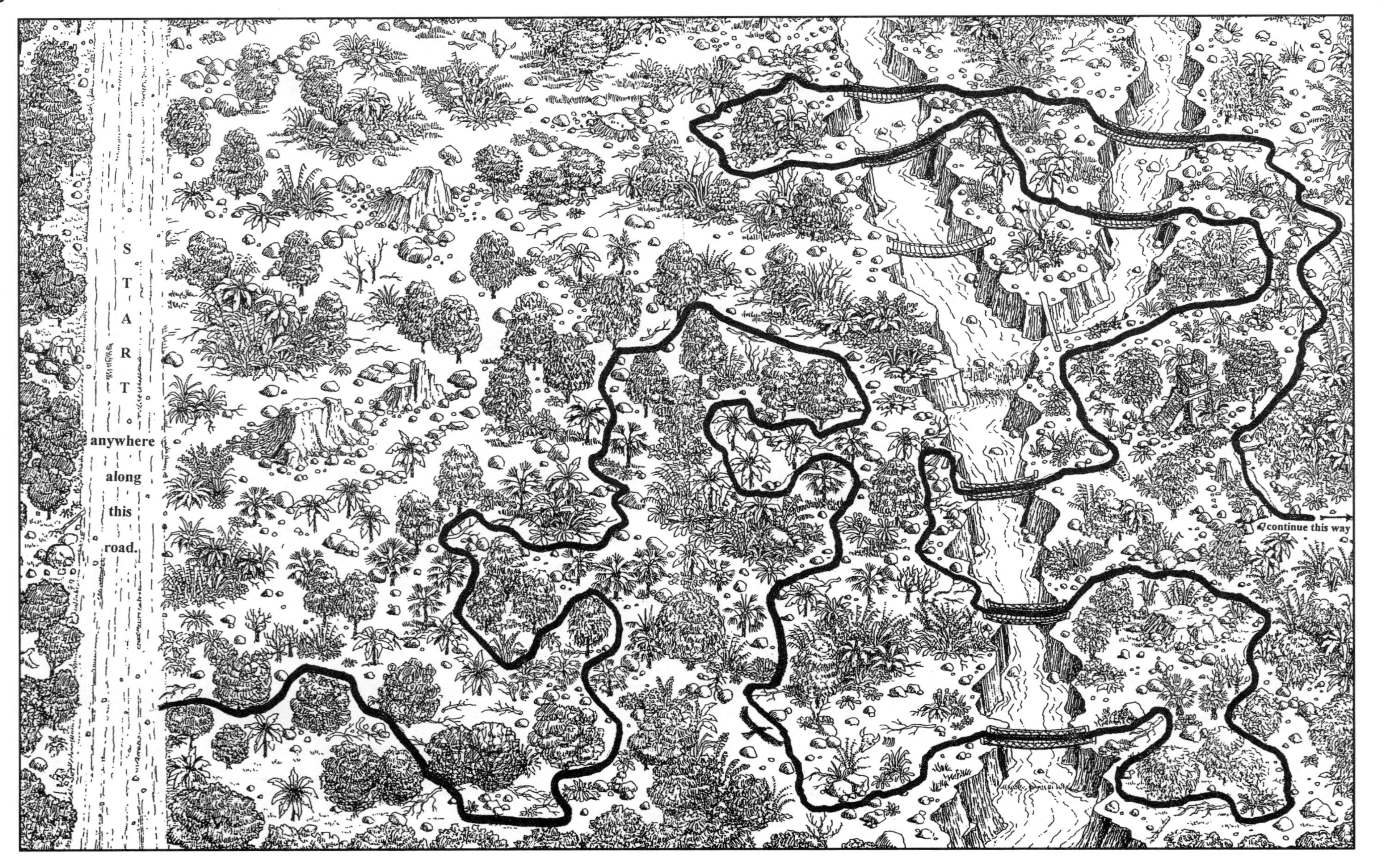

The Ruins

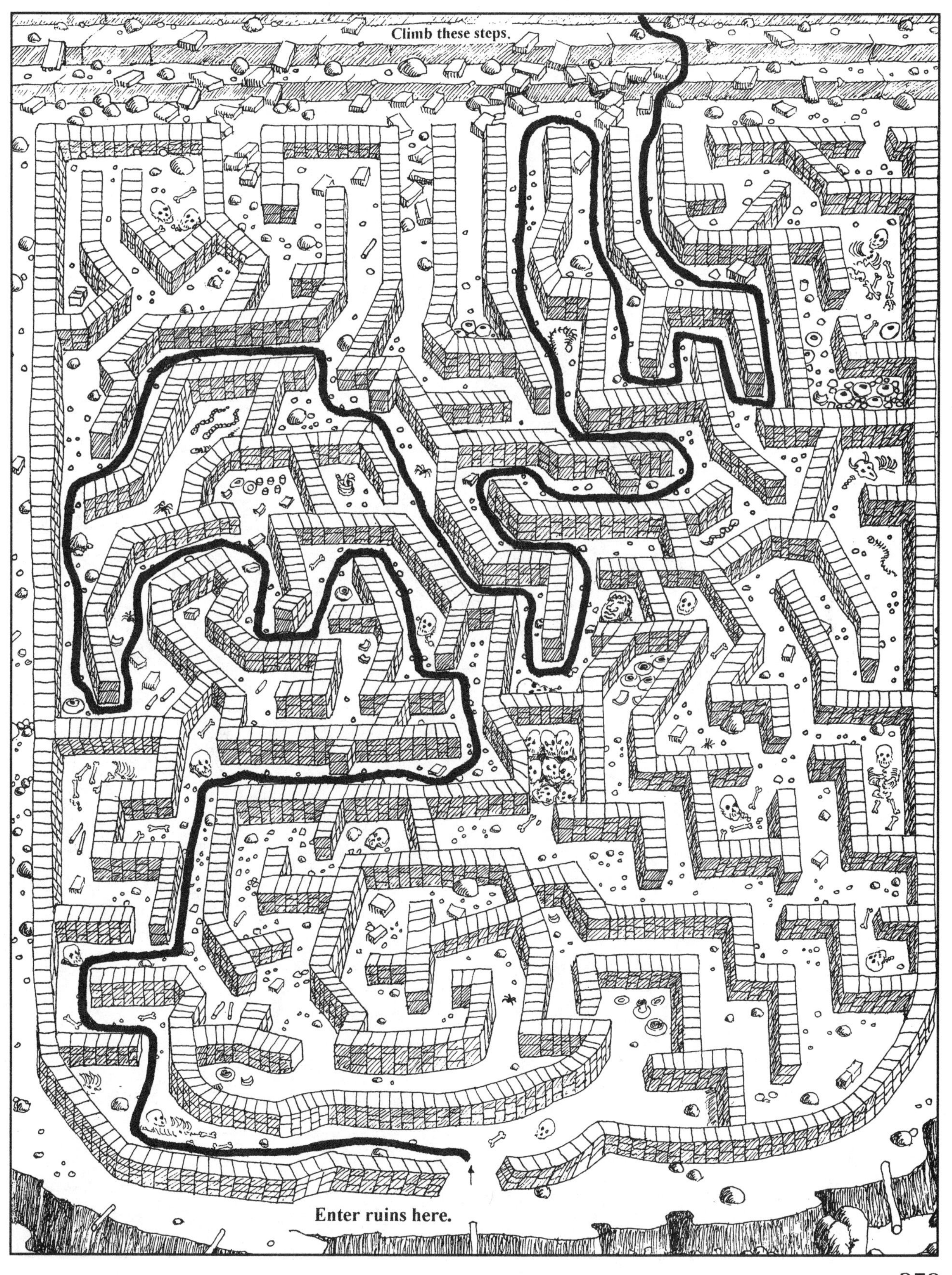

The Lost Mayan Temple

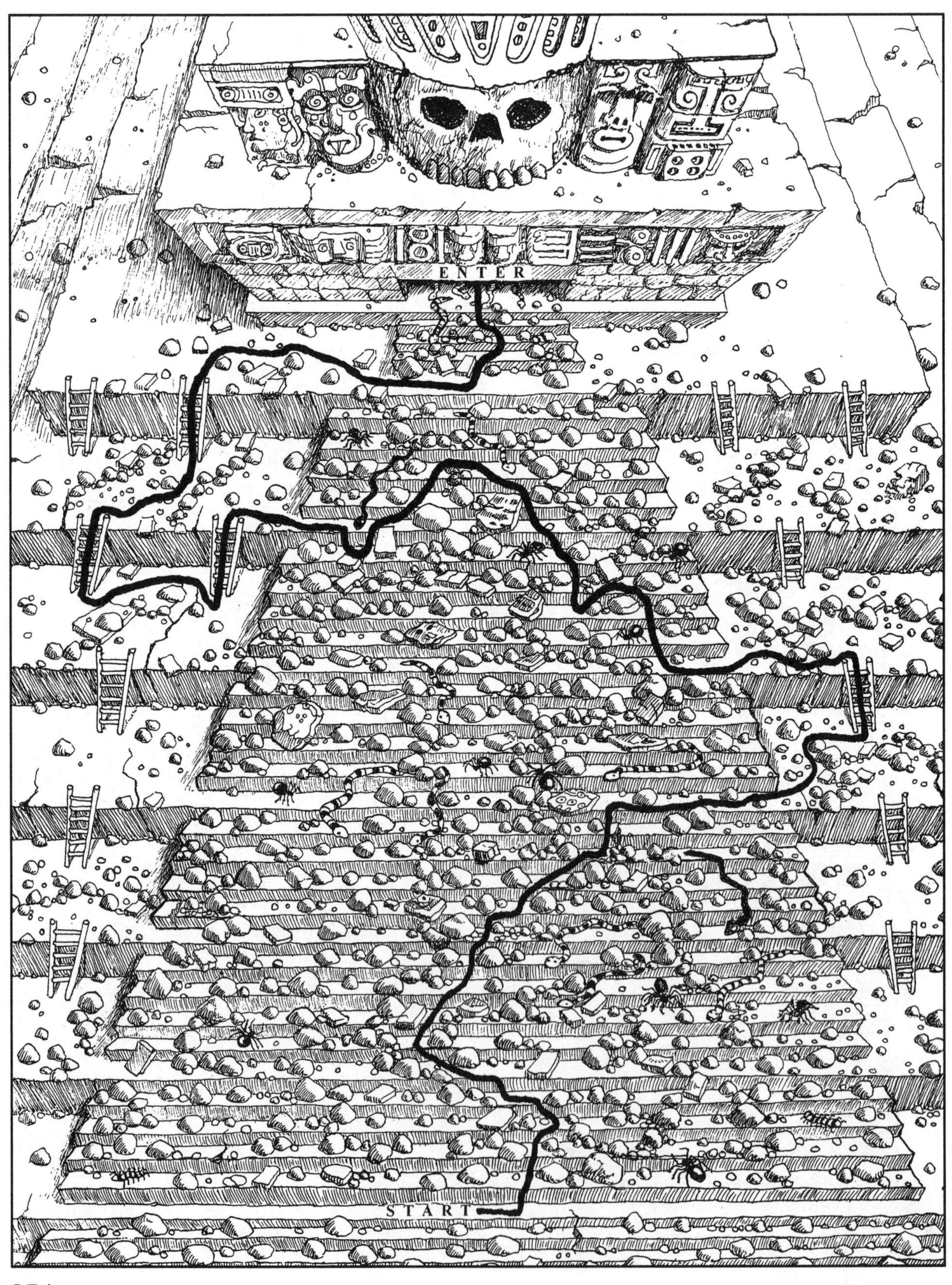

Oh No, Snakes

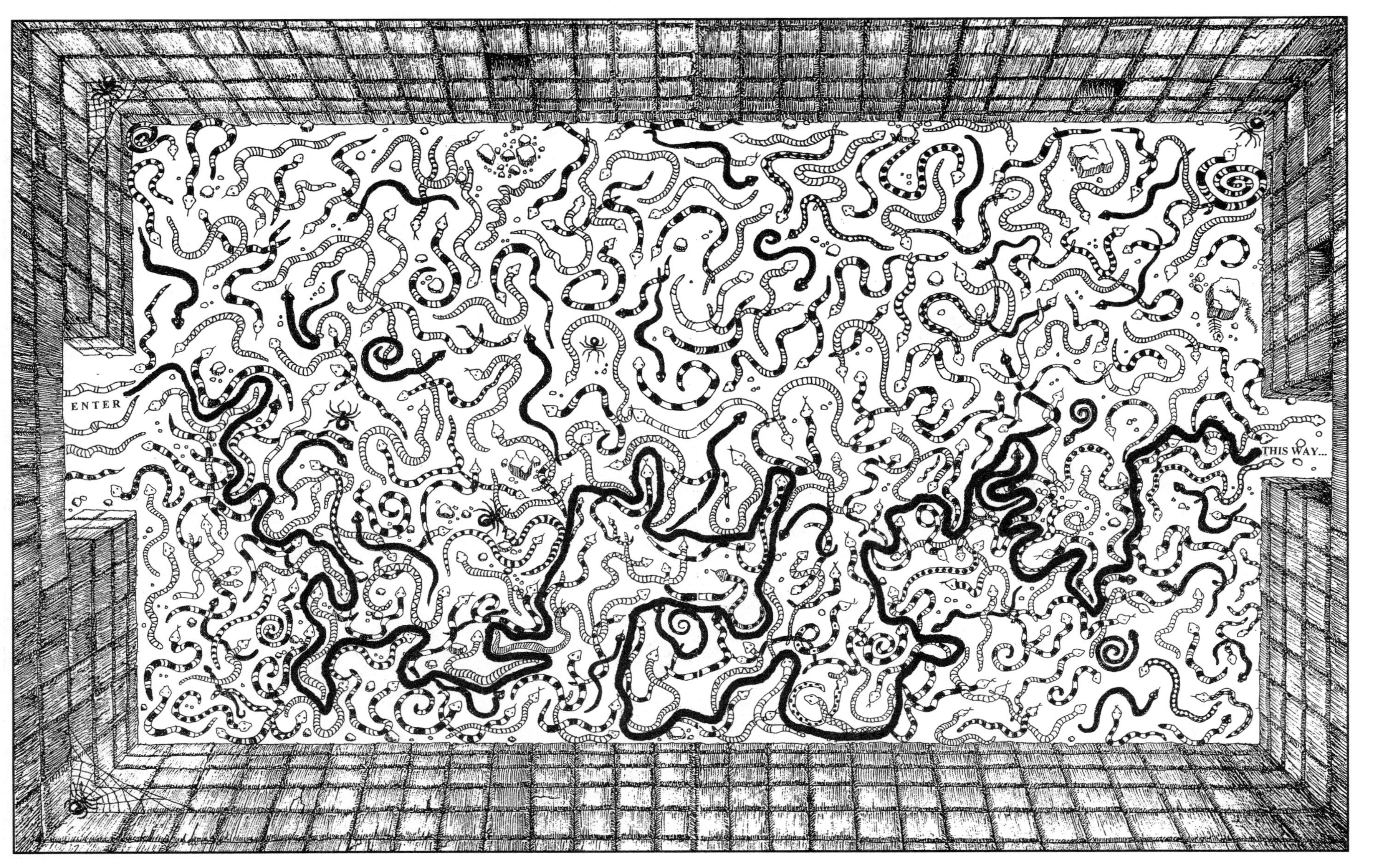

Exit through any of the 13 doors...if you can?
ENTER